W9-AAN-132

THE GOLDEN ROAD

THE GOLDEN ROAD

NOTES ON MY GENTRIFICATION

CAILLE MILLNER

THE PENGUIN PRESS

NEW YORK

2007

THE PENGUIN PRESS
Published by the Penguin Group
Penguin Group (USA) Inc., 375 Hudson Street, New York, New York 10014, U.S.A. · Penguin
Group (Canada), 90 Eglinton Avenue East, Suite 700, Toronto, Ontario, Canada M4P 2Y3 (a division
of Pearson Penguin Canada Inc.) · Penguin Books Ltd, 80 Strand, London WC2R 0RL, England ·
Penguin Ireland, 25 St Stephen's Green, Dublin 2, Ireland (a division of Penguin Books Ltd) ·
Penguin Books Australia Ltd, 250 Camberwell Road, Camberwell, Victoria 3124, Australia (a division
of Pearson Australia Group Pty Ltd) · Penguin Books India Pvt Ltd, 11 Community Centre,
Panchsheel Park, New Delhi – 110 017, India · Penguin Group (NZ), Cnr Airborne and Rosedale
Roads, Albany, Auckland 1310, New Zealand (a division of Pearson New Zealand Ltd) · Penguin
Books (South Africa) (Pty) Ltd, 24 Sturdee Avenue, Rosebank, Johannesburg 2196, South Africa

Penguin Books Ltd, Registered Offices: 80 Strand, London WC2R 0RL, England

First published in 2007 by The Penguin Press, a member of Penguin Group (USA) Inc.

Copyright © Caille Millner, 2007
All rights reserved

LIBRARY OF CONGRESS CATALOGING-IN-PUBLICATION DATA

Millner, Caille.
The golden road : notes on my gentrification / Caille Millner.
p. cm.
ISBN-13: 978-1-59420-109-7
1. Millner, Caille—Childhood and youth. 2. Millner, Caille—Family. 3. African Americans—
Biography. 4. Racially mixed people—United States—Biography. 5. African Americans—Race
identity—Case studies. 6. California—Race relations—Case studies. 7. Millner, Caille—Homes
and haunts—California. 8. African Americans—California—San Jose—Biography. 9. San Jose
(Calif.)—Biography. 10. African American women journalists—Biography. I. Title.
E185.97.M625A3 2007   2006051010

Printed in the United States of America
1 3 5 7 9 10 8 6 4 2

Designed by Marysarah Quinn

For my mother

CHAPTER ONE

MAYBE IT'S BEST TO BEGIN this story not when I learned I was black but when I learned I wasn't brown.

I learned this lesson in two stages. The second began on a Sunday morning in August of 1999. I was twenty years old, and I had spent the last several days and nights lying on a futon in my older brother's apartment. I was mute and insensate and I rose only for water and physical relief. My brother's wise response to this behavior was to ignore it, but on that particular morning he walked out of his bedroom and sat beside my head. He was going to mass, he said, and while he knows I am not Catholic he wanted me to go with him. In fact, I had agreed to go to mass several weeks ago. Perhaps I didn't remember that promise, he said—judging from my current state, that promise must have been made in a different epoch altogether—but he knows how I feel about promises.

I don't recall this agreement. But since I do feel a certain way about promises, I rolled off the futon and stepped headlong into an August morning in Los Angeles. Syrupy light ricocheted around my brother's cramped apartment in dust-drunk circles. Startling greens and blues from the trees and the sky—lurid colors too bright to be real—swam on the edge of my vision. Outside a chorus of car horns blared without mercy.

I was too delicate for all that. All that: Los Angeles; August; the final day with my brother, the culmination of a week we spent together in an effort to learn how to interact as adults. I wasn't sure the interaction effort was working, and I was afraid that might have been my fault. A passionate time in my life had come to an end, and although this was of no consequence to anyone, including, in the balance of things, myself, the shock temporarily crippled my emotional and physical responses. I did not sleep, I did not eat. I was so out of touch with my feelings that I could offer none to my brother. I merely made gestures at communication. And I had not brought any appropriate clothing for mass.

My brother rushed me. We don't want to be late, he said. Meanwhile he dropped his car keys and misplaced his shoes. He was nervous. He needed my approval. He needed me to respect his choice of church, his choice of religion, his choice of self, but I was not even looking respectable. I was bleary-eyed and forlorn, draped in a silk sundress that showed too much flesh, wishing for a shawl.

Whether I was respectable or not, mass must go on, and so I clung to the railing on the staircase leading down from my brother's apartment and folded myself into the passenger side of his car. The traffic was tight and restless. My brother fidgeted, swerved, cursed other cars. The parking lot of St. Augustine's Church was full when he pulled in, so we hunted for a space on the side streets while my brother yelled until tears welled up in his eyes. He'd wanted us to be here on time, not late as we always are. And now we are late, he said, and mass is ruined, because to walk into St. Augustine's after the priest has commenced worship is a sin on the order of blasphemy or fornication.

I considered this comparison as we lunged out of the car and raced into St. Augustine's, a palace composed in neo-Baroque fashion. The outside walls were whitewashed and the pillars were marble. It always looks absurd to create a full example of neo-Baroque architecture in Southern California, so a few ornate window carvings and gently extended buttresses sufficed, but as we approached the entrance I peered through the bright hard light to see that the Baroque spirit had triumphed inside. The walls and floor of the church were coral and sparkling. The wooden pews were polished to a high gleam. The altar appeared to have been dipped in gold, and the stained-glass interpretation of the Birth of the Lamb shattered the rainbow. As we approached I saw—because I was forced to see them, forced to push through them on my way inside—a small delegation of limbless beggars on the church steps. They lay on hospital cots, attended by an exhausted, flat-footed nurse. For each passerby they lifted up their heads and whined out a dreadful concert, in Spanish, for alms. A few of them rattled Styrofoam cups with a stump of arm.

The worshippers pushed through this corps without mercy. St. Augustine's was a brown church, upwardly mobile but still brown, a church that was less than one generation removed from poverty, a church with second mortgages on homes in Echo Park, a church that sent half its wages to Mexico, a church that wore twice-ironed whites. It was a church with a fierce anxious expression that had solidified while watching parents and brothers and friends rise at four in the morning for gardening jobs in Orange County. This was a church that knew how close it was to the squalor outside. A church that knew how dangerous it was to linger on the front steps.

This was a church, then, for Latin America, a church not unlike Santa Teresa in Mexico City or Igreja de São Francisco da Peniténcia in Rio de Janeiro. The fact that these worshippers were mostly Chicano—and by that I mean those who are of Mexican heritage but born and raised in the United States—was merely incidental. There were connections to the rest of Latin America here, connections that an outsider might not be able to see. They were connections that I recognized not because I was an insider but because before I was thirteen years old I learned my place in the world vis-à-vis the people who passed beyond this door. It was a necessary lesson in east San Jose, where my brother and I spent our childhood.

I probably would have learned no such lesson if we had grown up somewhere else. I might not have learned it even in some other part of California, as my parents would have wished. My parents did not plan to raise us in any part of San Jose. The chain of circumstances that led to their decision to move there was only one of the many situations for which my parents did not plan. Certainly the situation that surprised them the most was their own rapid ascent from impoverished, alcohol-sodden families into the upper middle class.

When I was a child, I asked my mother how they did it.

California made it possible for us, she said.

My mother is from a Creole family in Louisiana. Her mother's family traces its ancestry back to a slave woman named Sarah who found herself in a bit of a predicament when the father of her children, an Italian man who was also her master, went back to Europe with no warning. Sarah, who possessed quick wits as well as a keen understanding of how to use the chaos of a miscegenation-friendly French colony to her advantage, used a ruthless marriage strategy to establish her offspring in Louisiana's light-skinned Creole circles. There, she knew, her children would have access to enough financial freedom and personal security to allow them to live with a measure of dignity. Her strategy worked—the family acquired land and property and light-skinned, culturally approved offspring—until my great-grandmother fell in love with a dark-skinned black man named Alexander. She married him and was promptly disowned.

Penniless, they turned to sharecropping in central Louisiana. This was the profession they passed on to their children (including my grandmother Joyce) and their grandchildren (including my mother, Joyce). By the time Joyce II was five years old, she could pick fifty pounds of cotton a day. She spoke in Creole with an accent so thick that her own parents could barely understand her, but she did not allow the quizzical looks she received to keep her from asking questions. In fact, my mother's curiosity was notorious in her hometown of Palmetto. She got all of her whippings for pestering adults with questions or demonstrating in other ways what was then called sassiness.

When she wasn't being sassy, Joyce II would sometimes gaze at the postcards her mother kept in a hope chest next to her Bible.

Joyce I's twin sister, Eva, lived in Berkeley, and when Joyce I visited Eva, she returned with cards of the Golden Gate Bridge in San Francisco; the Half Dome glacier and the Mariposa Grove redwood trees in Yosemite National Park; Cypress Point in Monterey. She pulled those postcards out after we came home from church on Sundays, my mother said. They were creased in the middle and tattered at the edges, which made them that much more precious to both of us. She spread them on her quilt and we would stare at them and dream about the promised land.

Since the land was just a promise, my mother never expected to see it for real. She spent her days playing with her older brothers and sisters, helping her mother slop hogs and work in the truck-patch vegetable garden, learning her lessons when she could get to school, and alternately loving and fearing her father. Jean-Pierre, my grandfather, was the son of a fierce-tempered Native American father and a dark-skinned, French-speaking Creole mother. Everyone was afraid to go to their house, Joyce I said to me. Your grand-daddy's father was mean as hell every day of the week and twice as mean on Sundays.

Eventually everyone was afraid to go to Jean-Pierre's house, too, since he was known to shoot at his children and stab his visitors. But he only did these things when he was drinking. He worked three or four jobs simultaneously all of his life and never broke even, and the thought of facing life without alcohol was even more debilitating than the ruin he caused.

When he was sober he was quiet and loving, even indulgent. He once sat still and patient for an entire afternoon while my five-year-old mother tried to teach him how to read. Jean-Pierre died without learning how to read. He died before I was old enough to speak.

My mother was a nervous child, "delicate" in the same way her eldest sister is still called "delicate," as in fragile, easily stressed, prone to depressions. Living in a home where you must wake in the middle of the night in order to run through a cornfield and dive into a ditch to duck your father's bullets is unhealthy for the most stoic of us; it made my mother physically ill. School authorities, who knew all there was to know in a small town like Palmetto, told Joyce I that Joyce II needed to be removed from her living situation *immediately* and *permanently*, and Joyce I began to be afraid. As early as the day of my mother's birth, Joyce I had gotten offers and pleas from strangers—even white strangers, which was unheard of—to take and raise her beautiful baby. Since then, Joyce I had suspected that Joyce II would not be long in her care, but the possibility of losing her to Louisiana's foster care system was unthinkable. Joyce I spoke to her eldest daughter, Shirley, my aunt, the other "delicate" one. At eighteen Shirley had married an older man who was in the Army and moved to where he was stationed in Southern California. She had given birth to two children in quick succession, and the two women agreed that she could do with some help.

Joyce I packed Joyce II up and sent her to California on a Southern Pacific train. Joyce II was eleven years old.

But what am I supposed to do out there? Joyce II said when she heard that she was leaving. And how am I supposed to do it without you?

You just worry about helping Shirley take care of those babies, said Joyce I. And see if you can be a teacher. That's a good job for young ladies.

My mother rode alone in the train's colored car. She was too nervous to sleep and too homesick to eat, but she could still walk, and that is what she did when the conductor told her that she could move into the third-class car after they left Texas. No colored cars from that point on, he said. So go on, then. She blinked at these instructions, but for perhaps the first time in her life she had no questions. When the train left Texas she rewrapped her untouched fried chicken and pound cake in wax paper, and she picked up her cardboard suitcase and walked into the third-class car. When she got off the train in Santa Monica and saw the wide, paved streets, she knew that she had reached the promised land, but for many years she was gripped by a mother-hunger so strong that it did not matter. I didn't want to be in heaven if I couldn't bring her with me, my mother said. My whole life, I think, has been spent trying to figure out ways to bring her with me, even though I knew as soon as I got off the Southern Pacific that I had to do it alone.

Joyce II lived with Shirley and Shirley's family in the towns and cities of Santa Monica, West Covina, and Merced during the early 1960s. She was attending all-white schools, and she was living with a family that, while stable and generous, was not her own. Regarding both of these situations, she felt inadequate and ashamed. She also felt invisible, and one of her coping mechanisms for this particular feeling was to become invisible. She stopped asking questions. She studied hard at school and learned to be quiet and useful at home.

And in 1967, when her sister decided it was time for her to live with other relatives, she did not demand explanations. Perhaps by then the feelings of abandonment, dislocation, and mother-hunger had come to provide her with all the security she knew.

Joyce II moved to the Bay Area. She lived with Joyce I's twin sister, Eva, and her family in Berkeley. She attended Berkeley High School in 1967, 1968, and 1969, and it was there and then that her habits of silence, hard work, and conscientiousness made her visible, even exceptional. A guidance counselor named William Sherrill began to stand up for her. He arranged to have her placed in advanced courses instead of the remedial classes to which the administration routinely assigned black students. When she did well there, he called her into his office and suggested that she apply to college.

Try one of the California State University schools, Mr. Sherrill said. They've got something called the Master Plan. They're trying to educate students who wouldn't have had the opportunity to go to college even just a few years ago. They're cheap, for a college education, and they've got grants for people who don't have any money, as you may not.

My mother hadn't considered college. No one in her family had gone; she didn't even know what a college education might mean for her future. What she did know was that college cost money, and despite Mr. Sherrill's assurances, she was doubtful that any college acceptance board would understand just how little money she had. Still, by this point in her life she had decided that talking back or expressing doubt, in the form of asking too many questions, led to abandonment. She did not want to be lost by Mr. Sherrill. So she obeyed his orders to attend an informational meeting hosted by a San Jose State University recruiter, and it was there that she filled out her first and only college application.

Sometimes I wonder what would have happened to me if they had turned me down, my mother said. I wonder what I would have done after I graduated from high school, and how long it would have taken me to find out that I had to go to college if I wanted to be a teacher. Maybe I would have given up on being a teacher altogether. And I wouldn't have my two children.

But she was indeed accepted to San Jose State University. She graduated from Berkeley High School a semester early, spent the spring and summer of 1969 working as a fashion model to earn extra money, and in the fall of 1969 enrolled in her first courses. Eva, her husband, Faniel, and her daughter Ann drove with Joyce II sixty miles south on the Nimitz Freeway in a green Nash Rambler to help my mother move into her latest home. And as soon as they reached the campus—while Eva, Faniel, and Ann were still unpacking her clothes in her dorm room—my mother walked to the Educational Opportunity Program Office to make sure that her grants and loans were in order.

The student working behind the desk was my father.

My father was born in Columbus, Ohio, on April Fool's Day, 1946. His mother's family also traces its descent to a slave woman, Sabreth Johnson, who was abandoned by the white man who owned her and fathered her children. This white man, however, freed his mistress and his children and sent them away with three bags of gold. The three-bags-of-gold part of this story has a mythic ring to it, one of those bits of embroidery that exist in every family history, and I don't know if it was actually gold or three bags full, but shivers still run up my spine when I think about it. Whatever he gave her, it was enough for Sabreth to purchase 160 acres in Megs County, Ohio, and establish her family in the community of free blacks who lived there. Like the Creoles in Louisiana, the community in which my father's family lived was obsessed with skin color. Their marriage strategy was to bleach out as much color as possible, my father said. They got so good at it that many of them crossed the color line and never came back.

My father's father and mother both had hair that was just a little too curly for them to pass as white, but they had accepted the values with which they had been raised. If there is a rebel in that family when it comes to marrying for love, it is my father. He chose to marry a brown-skinned Southerner, exactly what he had been told to avoid by a long lineage of people who had clung to the lower rungs of Ohio's status ladder by following that time-tested advice.

But my father came of age in California. Time-tested advice, like time-tested history, has little purchase here.

My father's father, Charles Nelson, made the decision to move his wife and five children to California after being passed over for promotion again and again at his job with the U.S. Postal Service. (He passed the written exam every year, and every year he failed the interview portion as soon as he walked in and the testers saw that he was black.) At that time, in 1959, California had a free public university system, and Charles Nelson wanted his children to go to college and get the promotions that he had been denied. He was passionate about education. His own grandfather, a bootlegger named Will Dixon, attended Ohio State University for a year before his family's money ran out. While he was brewing beer and gin in the bathtub in his basement he would tell his seven-year-old grandson stories about the educated life with distant eyes and hushed tones, and as an adult Charles spoke to his children about college in the same way. He was less proud to talk to them about the other passion he had picked up from his grandfather, though they felt the damage all too keenly. Will Dixon employed his seven-year-old grandson as a runner. As Charles flitted through the woods that stretched between Columbus's neighborhoods, following those secret paths that only young boys can pick out, he paused behind the tree trunks to sample his deliveries. He loved alcohol immediately. By the age of seventeen he was a full-blown alcoholic, never leaving home without his fur coat and his silver flask, but he never allowed the habit to interfere with his reputation as a hard and diligent worker. It ruined his family life instead.

My father's mother, Barbara, was chronically depressed. She lost her mother at an early age and spent her childhood shuttling between family members, living with whoever could afford the emotional and financial strain of caring for one more relative. By the time she married and had children, she was horrified by the thought of further dislocation.

She came from what she called quality people, my father said. She took great pride in her lineage and had thoroughly researched her family history, maybe in part to get closer to the mother she would never see again. She had firm faith in manners and lineage and the idea of a society where everyone understood the mores and played within a set of rules. So you can imagine how much of a shock it was for her to come to California.

Barbara's depression and Charles Nelson's drinking fed each other. Their children watched mutely as their parents' battles escalated along a familiar trajectory; they noted, too, the costs. There were lost job opportunities (Charles Nelson failed his physical examinations at the local bus company and wound up back at the hated postal service, where he had to restart his career at the bottom of the seniority scale), lost social opportunities (the children could not invite their friends home for visits; Barbara could not entertain), and of course, the loss of whatever love had once existed between their parents.

Theirs is not a forthcoming family. I will never know what, exactly, it was in that home that created five children like my father, my uncles, and my aunt.

What I do know is that Charles Nelson's California dream came true for his children. All of them have had a formidable amount of education. As undergraduates, they attended California state universities; for their graduate work in law and chemistry and English and, in my father's case, sociology, they received scholarships to the finest universities this country has to offer. Three of them are tenured university professors; two are successful attorneys. What I also know is that they picked up a somewhat peculiar belief about family life. My father is the only son to have married. Two of my uncles are unrepentant bachelors with a distaste for monogamy; the third does not appear to date but lives in his parents' home in South-ern California and keeps it stocked with dozens of guns. When my aunt married, after claiming for many years that she never would, it was an enormous surprise; nor did my father get to the altar without a long struggle. And as my brother can attest, one of my father's constant refrains throughout our childhood was that he had never wanted to marry our mother or to have us.

When I grew up I confronted my father about this. He told me that he hadn't meant to imply that he didn't love us, his children, or our mother, as individuals. He simply hadn't wanted to get married or to have children, period.

I never meant for you to take it personally, my father said. I never even meant for you to hear it. Like a lot of things I've said, it came out all wrong.

Likewise, his opening sallies to my mother didn't flatter him. When they met in the Educational Opportunity Program Office, she thought he was the most arrogant man she had ever met. Nor was she impressed by the flirty notes he scribbled in the margins of her papers when he served as a teaching fellow in a class she was taking that first semester. To top it off, he had had some disastrous involvement with a good friend of hers from high school, who spent months yelling his name in conjunction with cuss words. In fact, my mother's first real conversation with him was an argument about said friend as my mother sprung to her defense.

How my mother got past this history to decide that he was the one for her is something I may never understand, but she did. At some point she looked past their inauspicious beginnings and cast her lot with him. She's told me that she admired his intellect and that she thought—because he was, and is, such an excellent teacher—that he would make a good father.

They were married in a Presbyterian minister's office on Claremont Avenue in Berkeley. It was 1972. They threw a wedding reception in their Telegraph Avenue apartment: two buckets of Kentucky Fried Chicken, a cake from Neldam's bakery in Oakland, four bottles of André champagne. My mother went shopping for her wedding dress alone—something that still makes her sad today—and she wore a beautiful purple dress, which she now feels may have been inappropriate.

I didn't know all the rules, she said. I should've worn white. I didn't know that traditionally brides wore color only if they were getting married a second time. I know that all those rules don't apply anymore . . . but I'm old-fashioned, I guess. Getting married was totally out of style in those days. If I was going to be out of style, I would've liked to go all the way.

They moved to San Jose because that was where my mother found a teaching position. They wanted to live in Berkeley; my father was studying for his Ph.D. at the University of California there, and my mother wanted to be close to Eva and Faniel. But none of the school districts were hiring in Berkeley, and while my father was a student my mother was the main breadwinner. They bought a single-story stucco house at 3427 Gila Drive in east San Jose, and they tried to build a family. It was slow going. I was born in 1979, and I still remember the arguments, which culminated in hours of screaming and occasional threats of violence. I remember the afternoons when my brother and I, just arriving home from preschool, would sit in front of my mother's closed bedroom door and whisper our plans to force her to stop weeping and come out. I remember the years, while I was in elementary school, when I visited my father in his rented rooms in other parts of town. I remember their lengthy separations. I remember meeting, often by accident, his other women, his other child.

For most of my life I hated my father because these were the only memories I allowed myself to have of him. He could do no right by me, and everything he said was a lie. My brother's relationship with our father was worse. None of us spoke to my father, and often our level of disgust was so high that we did not even speak to each other. Our home was a place of unearthly quiet; like all black people of a certain class, we were dreadfully concerned with respectability, and it would not have been at all respectable for us to fight openly, as perhaps we should have.

I changed my mind about my father the year I turned twenty-three. I had decamped to South Africa after an aborted mission to launch a communal-living arrangement in England with my boyfriend. I had already wasted the previous four years mooning about in one or another stage of heartbreak over different men, and during the months it took me to sort out the mental, emotional, financial, and spiritual morass I was in following this latest situation, I realized that it might be good for my love life, to say nothing of my sanity, if I tried to retrieve other memories of my father. So this time when my father reached out to support me, I did not shut him out. And I came to remember that he did reach out to me as a child. I remembered that he worked two and three jobs so that my brother and I could attend private schools, and that he invented games for us to play on long car rides. I remembered that he refused to pass on to his children any of the color consciousness that he had learned as a child. (Color consciousness, and an awareness of where I "fit" on the color scale, was not something that I even learned until I went to Harvard; in California I believed that there was black, there was white, and the distinctions ended there.) I remembered that I never saw him drinking, and now I remember that I must bring any man I believe may be worth dating to meet him: He knows all the games that men play, and if I am obedient, he will not allow any of them to be played on me.

We are a successful American family.

California made it possible for us.

I began this book to explore the idea that California could still make life possible for a family like mine. It was an attempt to wrestle with the different ways that California worked for my parents but did not work for my brother and me. California does not work for many people these days; but, then, maybe it never did. Maybe a close familiarity with that fact is what one needs to succeed here. Even in San Jose.

San Jose was and is a dull, faceless city. Most people who live outside California do not realize that it boasts more than a million residents and is the physical base of the American technology industry. Fifty years ago the city was prime property for the prune-growing business; perhaps as a result of this, San Jose has been unable to rid itself of the unfortunate tinge of provinciality, even when it was at the height of its cultural and economic power during the late 1990s. It is still seen as a far-flung suburb of San Francisco. This reputation is not helped by San Jose's sprawling development and demoralizing architecture: Almost every building resembles a suburban Elks hall. While I was growing up, one of the city's largest employers was IBM, but many IBM employees preferred to live in prettier places like Saratoga or Los Gatos. San Jose possessed few attractions—a destitute theater company, the hopeless downtown shopping promenade, the spooky Rosecrucian Egyptian Museum— to keep them there.

But San Jose did attract large communities of ethnic minorities, including the second-largest Vietnamese population outside Vietnam. In the 1980s east San Jose was a polyglot mix of Vietnamese, Filipinos, Japanese, Koreans, lower-middle-class whites, a few blacks, and—especially—Latinos, who in 1980 represented 22 percent of the city's population. By 2000 they represented 30 percent of San Jose; African Americans claimed 5 percent.

But these are merely numbers; they mean nothing to a child. The only thing I understood, growing up in my part of San Jose, my neighborhood, my street, was that the children I played with and fought with and learned from weren't black. The parents whose homes I entered and whose tables I ate at—those people weren't black either. But these were the people who gave me my first idea of what it meant to live as a person of color in the United States. *Spics*, the children at my middle school taunted them. *Greasers. Messikens.* And my first stirrings of racial consciousness, my first awareness of prejudice and the variety of responses to that prejudice, weren't based on what black Americans call "the struggle." They were linked to a different, more ambiguous understanding, a history more or less alienated from white America, a code of humiliations and humilities that can be summed up in two words: *la lucha*.

And because I grew up with *la lucha*, I didn't just grow up with the neighborhood's vision of American history—a history that seemed to begin with the Treaty of Guadalupe Hidalgo, only to swerve and dip among Homestead Acts and zoot suits and *bracero* programs to reach its culmination in the figure of Cesar Chavez— I grew up with the neighborhood's culture as well. Or perhaps I should say I grew up familiar with it. For my first lesson was to learn that I never really got past the door.

MY BROTHER AND I pushed past the threshold into the church. As we stormed in he plucked a bit of holy water from a stand and crossed himself. Then he grabbed my arm and thumped into a pew at the back of the church. This is where we sat, since he decided that in the course of a four-year Catholic-school education I had not been properly educated on the procedures for mass. I sat. I folded my hands in my lap. My brother knelt beside me and pressed his fists into his brow. All around me, people knelt, murmured, hummed. Some wandered around the church, dabbing themselves with holy water, pausing at saints' statues. At the door, those who were presumably unconcerned by blasphemy and fornication walked in, their shoes clattering on the coral tile. The grim-faced priest was at his labors with the jugs of wine, the platters of wafers, the leather-bound books. I sat. I watched. So this is what goes on beyond the door.

As a child I spent my Sundays at Emmanuel Baptist Church, a stucco cavern some twenty minutes and two or three worlds away from our house. Our mother was quite open to the diverse backgrounds of our friends, but she had her cultural requirements, one of which was that her children would grow up in a black church. So every Sunday morning, while our friends went off to mass—which was in my imagination less a church service than a brief carnival of elaborate prayers and lacy clothing—my brother and I went to Emmanuel.

The congregants who filled Emmanuel every Sunday came from all over the Bay Area. Nearly all of them were born and raised in California but were determined to preserve a black Southern Baptist image of church, an image that many had received from their parents and grandparents and their faint inklings of atavistic memory, and that some had received from television. But since it was so removed from the historical context it sought to emulate, Emmanuel was a parody of everything Americans associate with black Baptist churches. So there were the four-hour services. There was the enormous choir clad in bathrobes. There were the fainting scenes every month. There was the pastor, a huge man with a Jheri curl, who wore white suits with pink suspenders and pink spats and drove a Cadillac. Some actual worshipping may have gone on there, but I am not the one to ask. My brother and I came home on Sunday afternoons feeling lost and bewildered, eager to shake off the bizarre ordeal and our envy of the other children, who had been playing in the streets for hours. Neither my brother nor I really made any friends at Emmanuel.

There were two other black households on our block. One of them was an older woman who lived alone. Paula kept a crumbling canary-yellow house with no lawn. A chain-smoker, hideously wrinkled, deathly quiet but for occasional outbursts, she was our most feared neighbor. Those outbursts alternated between domestic disputes with her boyfriends and attempts on her own life. Both scenarios tangled the streets with yellow tape for hours. Our mother warned us to stay away from her, but no such precaution was necessary. All the children weaved around the orbit of her house in half-moons. Nor did any of the children associate with the other black household, where no adults seemed to be present. With the exception of Ingrid, a tall, graceful girl who spoke gently and inhabited a soft, dreamy space, the house consisted of intimidating teenagers. One of them, Jason, robbed my family blind while babysitting my brother and me.

Neither my brother nor I really made any black friends at all.

This became a problem when our mother decided it was time to teach us what she knew we would need for our emotional and psychological survival: the history of black people in America. She knew she was fighting against the currents of everything we would face for the rest of our lives—the indifference of main-stream culture, the entrenched subtleties of white racism, the devastation of black self-hatred—and she tackled her task accordingly. She crammed our bookshelves with histories of slavery and the civil rights movement. She selected our books for school reports, inevitably biographies of Harriet Tubman or George Washington Carver. She organized weekend trips to Oakland, where our father dutifully pointed out the site of Huey Newton's murder. She read us Langston Hughes's poetry at bedtime and played Motown records after dinner. She bought us T-shirts printed with black heroes and power slogans. And she taught us, mostly by example, the importance of forcing a black presence into every possible milieu. Each February brought dramatic scenes in the offices of our clueless elementary school principals. Our mother would march in and demand to know what the school was doing for Black History Month. Did they have their posters, their announcements, an assembly? Did they need materials? She could recommend some and, if asked properly, could even loan them to the school for the season.

But there was one thing she could not do, and that was make the history come alive for her children in their bubble of east San Jose, the bubble of *banda* music and Western Union cables to Mexico. Because I was young and black people were in short supply, the history of black people in America felt foreign, thrilling, even a little exotic. Shackles and chains! Freedom by the North Star! White riots! Bull Connor! Black American history was a catalog of spectacular atrocities to rival the history of early Christians in the Roman Empire—and it felt about as far away. Whereas the history of *la lucha* taking place around me was a history of misery and regret, of silent anger, a series of small daily humiliations that left everyone ragged at the seams. A history of ambiguity: the ambiguity of the migrant workers shivering outside McDonald's at five o'clock in the morning, of the Norteño gangs and their coats of many colors, of the free-trade agreements, of the border itself. The American history that books and T-shirts and posters are unable to capture, much less explain, that is the history of mundane misery.

CULTURALLY SPEAKING, I had what will soon become the American childhood, a mélange of cheerful American pragmatism and Latin baroque and African-American skepticism. The hybridity seemed irreconcilable for so many years until I understood the American habit of maintaining a reductive naïveté through compartmental-ized guilt. I hadn't yet learned to feign ignorance toward the different parts of myself, to participate in national innocence through collective delineation. Until I understood this, it was impossible for me to integrate my childhood memories.

At every birthday party a piñata, the beating of which heralded rips and grass stains on massive white dresses. Sporadic attendance at mass, but baptisms and first communions requiring a rented public space and a mariachi band. At least three cars to every house: two beached in the driveway or on the curb, one without wheels. Every Saturday afternoon, a team of oil-stained men surrounding the cars, fortified by a cooler of beer and a beat-up radio booming Mexican rock. Scant mention of Mexico in school history classes; still, a regular festival for Cinco de Mayo (but only those aspects that could be safely dehistoricized and commodified, such as *folklórico* performances and trays of empanadas), which was much more fun than Martin Luther King Jr. Day (always a dreary assembly, with the tone-deaf lower grades crooning "We Shall Overcome" to a piano arrangement that sounded like a dirge). Long, bedazzling days of fruit-picking in Watsonville with friends' families. Childish beauty fantasies guided by the hands of older Chicanas, who insisted on the elegance of black lip liner and Aqua Net hair spray. Cafeteria burritos on Monday, tacos on Thursday. Innumerable aunts and cousins in every family, and at least four godparents for every child. All-night story sessions when *la abuela y la tía* came to visit. First crushes named Cruz. A Spanish vocabulary consisting exclusively of cuss words and slang. Slip 'n Slides, kiddie pools, and jugs of Kool-Aid dragged out to front yards during hot summer nights. Parents drunk enough on the heat and the long conversations to slosh in the pools by midnight. Joking discussion of *la dueña* when the prettiest daughters started to date. Family photographs on every available surface. Letters from Mexico. The rosary. Black beans. Gilt.

Were I to draw a timeline, the list would end during the summer after my first year of middle school. I can place an exact moment, in fact: a hot July evening during the summer of 1991.

That was the night I discovered a cheerful rap group from Los Angeles. My teacher in rap, as in so many things that summer, was a girl named Indiana. We were constant companions. Our friendship was based on our shared inability to join any acceptable clique at school. Indiana was wiry and nervous and possessed of a schizophrenic beauty. It was the nervousness, and the fact that she was *flaca* at a time when most Chicanas were developing curves, that kept her locked out of the group she desired to join. She was also unsuitable—though I didn't realize this at first—because she was not really Chicana but some inexplicable white ethnic mix that failed to make the cut. I was withdrawn into myself even then, socially awkward, and far too developed for anyone's good. We made an interesting pair that summer, cruising the mall, begging our mothers to leave us unchaperoned at the amusement park, stealing candy and cigarettes from the pharmacy.

One Friday night, an uncle or cousin or one of Indiana's mother's boyfriends—there were always men at Indiana's house, men who were gruff and burly, men whose clothes shone with permanent grease stains—announced his intention to drive through east San Jose in order to pick up a spare part for his car. Indiana wheedled him into taking us along. The wait for the spare part would be long and stifling and he would threaten to abandon us before it was all over, but we knew that before we drove off, and we knew, too, that it would be worth it. He had to drive down Santa Clara Street.

During the week, Santa Clara Street was a six-lane road connecting a mercantile stretch of east San Jose (*panaderias*, pool halls, tattoo parlors) with one downtown (flagship investment banks, high-rise hotels) and the Rose Garden district (historical-society homes, attorney-at-law offices, parking regulations). Then it passed the 87 freeway and became the Alameda. The Alameda ran into the netherworld of Santa Clara (Santa Clara University, gourmet coffee shops, weekend farmers' markets). So the street attracted all types of people. But many of those people stayed far away from the east San Jose side on weekend nights.

Because when the weekend came, the cars came out of hiding. Long, sleek, candy-colored machines with fantastical names like LeBaron and Eldorado and Monte Carlo. Cars with periwinkle interiors and sparkling headlights. Suicide doors, Daewoo speakers piled in the back, whitewall tires, rearview mirrors draped with green pine trees, embroidered Mexican flags, rosary beads. Twenty-inch rims. The license plates read LINDA and MAMI and SANCHA, and the trunks told an airbrushed story about La Morenita, the Virgin of Guadalupe, re-envisioned with buxom curves and a ripped red bodice to match her sheaf of roses. These were cars that demanded the sacrifice of every Friday afternoon for polishing, cars that insisted upon trips to Richmond or Daly City for the special mechanics who could make them bounce. These were exacting vehicles, and what they exacted on Santa Clara Street was a traffic flow of about five miles an hour.

So there we were. Our driver was thirty-five years old, with two jobs, two kids, and a gambling habit. He had no patience for Santa Clara Street. He snarled and honked and ducked in and out of lanes. Our vehicle was a rust-colored hardtop, completely at odds with protocol. But although we were ashamed, neither Indiana nor I expected anything else. We knew that Santa Clara Street was not for the likes of us. Content to be in the crush, the excess, the sweat, the beauty, the noise, we pushed to each side of the bench seat in the back and hung our heads out the windows.

That's when I heard "On a Sunday Afternoon" approaching from a red Sentra on our right. Sentras were not designed to cruise—they were Japanese, for one thing, and aesthetically they were far too small and boxy—but this one was trying its best, with gleaming rims, tinted windows, and a sound system blaring the song of the moment. I was enthralled: The song's focus was a rolling barrio voice, which looped and hopped down one of the melodies I had heard so many times from my mother's Motown collection. I asked Indiana about the song, and she shoved over to my side. The song, she said after a moment's listening, was enormously popular on all the local radio stations. Everyone she knew from our school was listening to it, and she heard it everywhere she went—in shopping malls, parking lots, corner stores. She was amazed that I hadn't heard it before. Maybe, she said, such silliness could be explained by the name of the group in question, A Lighter Shade of Brown, and the fact that by choosing such a name, they were saying that they were a shade too dark for her and a shade too light for me.

THAT'S ONE VERSION of my first lesson.

An alternate version also begins the summer after I turned twelve, the summer I spent trying to decipher my first year of middle school. It had been wretched, as adolescence can be; it had been academically shocking, as California public schools can be; it had been socially torturous, as time among a collection of children with too much money and too little supervision can be. Part of the problem was certainly me. My family had recently moved out of east San Jose into the Almaden Valley. With my father's expanding job prospects—after graduating from Berkeley, he joined San Jose State as an assistant professor and earned tenure as a full professor in a startlingly short time—my parents began looking for ways to improve prospects for their children. They immediately latched onto the idea of moving into a neighborhood with better schools than east San Jose's. By all objective standards, Almaden Valley was better: a hushed, tree-lined neighborhood where the streets were clean and the supermarkets were stocked and the neighbors avoided one another. There were no children my age in the neighborhood, not that I would have seen any who might have lived there. People did not venture out of doors. So I did not receive a proper introduction to the children of Almaden Valley until my first year at Bret Harte Middle School.

They were terrifying. Their voices were flat and starched, with blunt edges that popped every possibility of curvature and melody. The sentences those voices spoke prickled with colloquialisms like *tool* and *wicked* and *awesome*. The word *like*, which I had always understood was to be used strictly for comparative purposes, functioned in their language as a partitive article. They wore polo shirts tucked into tight, cuffed jeans, and they accessorized with high-top sneakers and crimped hair. I was appalled. I was even more appalled when I saw the way they treated the children from east San Jose—the children who had been bused in, reeking of poverty and defiance—as a criminal class of aliens. They were only children and yet they had already absorbed the lessons of Almaden Valley. They already understood which groups must remain outside their doors.

But I found no comfort in the company of outcasts either. Perhaps it was because I had moved. Already when we visited the old neighborhood I sensed hostility. My friends' parents—the adults who had guided my hands to make enchiladas and joked about boyfriends (*morenita linda*, they teased me, and only now did I consider that being called the pretty little dark one could mean many things, not all of them complimentary)—ignored me or, worse, treated me with false cordiality. Most of the children I grew up with did not attend Bret Harte. They were resigned to middle schools in the eastern districts or bused to other locales around the city. The few who did attend my school made it clear to me that perhaps we shared a common history and context but not a common address or color. I walked home; they boarded the bus. And—the insult, the final judgment—I may have grown up Chicana, but I was not, after all, *a* Chicana.

It was this last fact that devastated me. The move was unfortunate, but it was out of my control. Nor was it, in itself, irreconcilable. A few weeks in Almaden Valley were enough to teach me that no one would stop me if I resisted integration into my new neighborhood. And even if the move did change everything, even if it was solely a question of my address—perhaps if their exclusion had been based on that, and the heavy baggage of class and betrayal, I could have accepted it.

But to lose my childhood friends over something that was so far out of my control that it was also out of my comprehension, something that had, until now, existed for me solely in books and the month of February—that was overwhelming, and I reacted badly. When I met the cold stares of children I had known since preschool, children who I knew would still cry at the drop of an ice-cream cone, I did not stare back. I shrank. When my tentative greetings were rebuffed, I did not repeat them with more strength. I kept moving. And because I did not force my old friends—and their new friends—to face the pain of their rejection, I excused their behavior. I let them believe they were right. I let them believe that being un-Chicana really was appropriate grounds for dismissal. And I let them see only my shame.

On the other hand, I realized that with their rejection came a kind of grace. From my new perspective I watched the children I once knew change into something unrecognizable. They boasted about their graffiti skills and the number of school days they had cut. They developed cravings for alcohol and tobacco. They spent their time at the San Jose Boxing Club, either fighting or cheering for their boyfriends. They *had* boyfriends—and the hickeys to prove it. They wore clothes that seemed to be chosen as an affront not just to the local community but to anyone who might approach them with a friendly smile. The boys favored white tank tops tucked into over-sized canvas jeans. The jeans were covered with white topstiching, and they cinched them at the hip with well-tooled leather belts. They clomped around in work boots and frowned from beneath their spiderweb *malla* hairnets, but the best accessory was a girl-friend, clad in black leggings and her boyfriend's Starter jacket. In case their boyfriends were not fearsome enough, the girls armored themselves every morning with a visage so extraordinary as to border on both the medieval and the futuristic: a pale, white-powdered face matched with bloody lips and slashes of black eyeliner, all rising from beneath a lacquered shell of long bangs bent above their heads in a concentric arc. In this costume they roamed the halls, always in packs, always louder than everyone else.

And as I watched them, and watched the school administration take what was called appropriate measures—banning virtually every item of clothing they wore in the name of decorum, segregating them into ESL classes without so much as a language test, fighting new busing measures—I wondered whether it was perhaps too quaint of me to ask what had happened to the principles I had learned as a child, the principles of *la lucha*. Soon I was to understand that the children I once knew had just gotten there ahead of me. Their idea of honoring *la lucha* was to exclude those who did not, and never would, understand the ambiguity of their lives. There was no need to struggle with the principles of Bret Harte and Almaden Valley when they could make a perfectly acceptable community unto themselves. Even if they had to exclude someone they once knew, as swiftly and effectively as they had been excluded. It was not personal. They were just exercising that age-old survival technique for people of color, a technique I was soon to exercise myself. The creation of public and private selves, wholly separate and wholly exclusionary.

THROUGH MY REJECTION I learned the paranoia and self-doubt of the black American middle class—I learned the typical response to a lifetime of the subtle slights I endured that first year of middle school. Snubs and whispers and disacknowledgment can be more devastating than outright humiliation, at least if I am to compare my progress with that of my friend Jaime.

I had heard of Jaime long before I met him. Or perhaps I should say I had heard about him, because everyone at Bret Harte heard what the Chicanos thought of Jaime. If they spotted him in the halls, loud laughter was sure to follow. Then the daily dissection began. His pants fit wrong. His hair looked as though it had been cut with hedge clippers. He wore the wrong colors—a trangression that could get you attacked by gangs in some neighborhoods, but it was taken for granted that no one could possibly be insulted by Jaime. How could they? He spoke funny. He lived in the wrong neighborhood—not east San Jose, but south of Almaden Valley, near Gilroy, where his father worked on the garlic farms. He ate tortillas with lard—like he still lived in Mexico, the taunt went. This, of course, being the real problem: Jaime was not a Chicano. He was a recent immigrant, a Mexican-from-Mexico.

Perhaps the real problem included the fact that Jaime was so determined to get out of ESL classes that he studied English on his own time. I first met him in the library after school. He was propped behind an English grammar book, mouthing the words to himself. He did get out of ESL in the eighth grade, and I remember watching him in art class, smiling at the teacher, at all the students, smiling, in fact, at everyone, out of simple pride at his own presence. Perhaps the real problem also had to do with Jaime's refusal to keep up with the Chicanos' fashion and lingo and lifestyle. All those things cost too much money, he said when I asked him why he did not wear top-stitched jeans or a Starter jacket. He wore his grass-stained T-shirts and his close-fitting pants without embarrassment or apology. Nor did he feel badly about missing dances and parties. They too cost money, but even more than that, they cost emotional capital, and Jaime had other plans for that. He invested his energy in cultivating a friendship with a boy named Darren, one of the richest boys at Bret Harte.

Darren responded to Jaime with the peculiar curiosity of the benevolent rich toward the ambitious poor. Jaime was smart and industrious, and that was impressive, but he was also different from the Chicanos—*his father works on a garlic farm? he studies English on his own time? he eats tortillas with lard?*—and that was even more impressive. Darren was impressed enough to invite Jaime to Lake Tahoe for a weekend with his family.

The invitation sparked fevered gossip all over school. The children of Almaden Valley were mystified. They had never noticed Jaime and saw no reason for Darren to notice him either. The Chicanos were irritated, dismissive. In loud hallway discussions they made it clear that they would never go skiing—snow, broken legs, and all those white people. Jaime was not bothered by the snow or the broken legs or the white people, and he returned from the trip with a goggle sunburn and a newfound confidence in himself. He shared his story of victory on the bunny slope with anyone willing to listen.

Darren was equally eager to share his memories of the weekend. Students asked him, as quietly as they could, what it was like to host Jaime. Surely he had done something strange, like bring tortillas with him. But to such inquiries Darren responded only with laughter. Jaime had a great time, he said. Jaime was kind and charming, and Darren's parents were impressed that he had made friends with such a sensible young man. His father had spoken to Jaime at length about his interests and his future plans, and the possibility existed that his father would advise Jaime about some of the professions that Darren was considering. His father had mentioned this, in fact, after watching Jaime exhibit the only example of odd behavior of the trip. Jaime had spoken extensively to the maids and servers at the ski lodge, in Spanish, and he had done the same thing with the men who worked on the ski lift. It was not odd behavior in and of itself, Darren corrected himself, it was just not something he would do. But he believed Jaime's behavior was perfectly understandable since, as his father said, Jaime would probably wind up working at a place like that himself.

Perhaps the real problem was not that Jaime overstepped his boundaries. Perhaps it was that Jaime did not understand his boundaries—that he believed in the idea of America so much that he did not recognize where he was supposed to be and where Darren was supposed to be and where the Chicanos were supposed to be and where I was supposed to be. He did not recognize that these four groups represented distinctive categories and should not be mixed except in situations of necessity or duress.

Perhaps the real reason was that Jaime did not understand America, at least the America I was coming to understand.

AT TWELVE YEARS OLD, my own private self devastated, I went in search of a public one. Naturally, I began my search in books. But not just any books: the same books that crammed my bookshelf at home and were selected for my school reports, the same books that my mother waved around in the principal's office every February. The same books that, in my young eyes, bore some responsibility for my rejection. I began with them, in the hope that if they possessed the power to take away they might also possess the power to give.

So at the age of twelve I read *The Autobiography of Malcolm X*, the book that startled me, as it has startled so many people, into consciousness. Malcolm's brilliance was my entrée into an amazing world of apocalypse, of fire and brimstone, of hellfire. Here, finally, was the language of prophecy, of the Southern black preachers' tradition. Here was the passion that was missing from the pulpit of Emmanuel Baptist Church, wrought into the neatest symmetry possible. There was no ambiguity in Malcolm's words. There was no *quincesada*, no truancy, no Cinco de Mayo, no rosary. There was nothing of *la lucha*. There was black, there was white, and there was a choice. That was all.

It was a simplicity I found comforting for the next several years. But Malcolm's words were for the black American in the South, the black American of my mother's childhood and Malcolm's own childhood, living in a state of hopeless rage under brutal circumstances of poverty and segregation. And his words were for the black American in the Northern industrial metropolis—Philadelphia, New York, Detroit, Chicago—seething in mute fury at the black ghetto he lived in, and at the destitution and racism that kept him there. As deeply as I felt his words, they were not designed for the black American west of the Mississippi, flailing with confusion halfway between the childhood vision of a brown world (Latin, baroque, stylized despair, a shrug) and the encroaching reality of a white one (Anglo, austere, frantic, a blank stare). Without the presence of a black community I was on my own for daily interpretation.

How to construct a self between those three worlds: the brown, the white, and the new consciousness of the black (without, of course, the human proof)? Did I even need the first two worlds—the ones that had, consciously and unconsciously, already shown me the futility of my position? What if I just chose the world (without, of course, the human proof) I knew only from books?

I chose.

With the culture chosen, I set about creating the community. Because this is a California story, I sought out answers not only in books but also on television and in the movies. These media nearly always have an answer—nearly always the wrong answer, but then I was attempting to create a self with the guidance of a book. Wrong answers did not disturb me. What, I asked in my increasingly bitter thoughts, had I created myself upon for all these years but wrong answers?

So without irony I turned to television and the movies for advice about what type of self I should create. I could not have picked a better time to look. It was the early 1990s, and what I saw in the media was the vision of other young people drawing attention to their interpretation of the struggle. There was tremendous anger and rebellion in black youth culture during those years—those brief moments of Public Enemy and Afrocentricism and Spike Lee—and that excited me. It excited me to know that other young people were dissatisfied with a birthright of suffering and victimhood. It excited me to see them fighting it. I too began to fight, in the small ways I could: I slipped out of my house to join the local protests against the Rodney King verdict in 1992. I joined my mother in the principal's office every February. I made a point of staying seated, reading Malcolm or *They Came Before Columbus* or *Native Son*, every morning during the Pledge of Allegiance. These gestures made me feel as though I too had a struggle for which I could legitimately fight. Because that is what I felt. I had similar feelings of fury and rebellion (but at what, I ask now—just what did I know to be furious and rebellious toward?), and so I imagined myself a member of the community I saw on television. But communities make demands on their members, and without that human presence I could only look to the television to discover of what those demands might consist.

Buy, said the television, as televisions do. So I filled my private spaces with the music and clothing of my imagined community. My acquisition of these things was as misguided as my advisor. I dragged my mother to every international festival listed in the newspaper. Baffled, she watched as I tore through the booths of dreadlocked white hippies in search of my treasures. Perhaps because they were cheap, and perhaps because she was relieved I was not asking for midriff tops and short skirts as other girls my age were, she bought me the head wraps and the (made-in-China) kente cloth without complaint. She even took me to Oakland, where I searched through three black barbershops until I found a medallion engraved with the shape of Africa.

The music was a different story. My mother refused to let most rap albums enter her house. Filth, she said. And degrading to women. So I did what most Almaden Valley children did: I went to Nick.

Nick was a towheaded seventh grader with green eyes and a splash of freckles across his nose. He lived in an enormous house in the Almaden hills, and in addition to wealth, he enjoyed the blessing of parental indulgence. They bought him whatever he asked for, even the albums with the pesky PARENTAL ADVISORY labels that unaccompanied children were restricted from purchasing. Nick loved rap music, especially the aggressive sounds coming out of Southern California. He was the fastest runner in my class, and during physical education class he raced coolly around the track, belting lyrics at the top of his voice—

Knowin' nothin' in life but to be legit
Don't quote me boy cuz I ain't said shit

—he sang and he pumped his small fist in the air.

Thanks to his parents' lenience, Nick had access to music that was kept away from the rest of us. So in true entrepreneurial fashion, he launched a home business. He made himself available for requests and copied his albums for a small fee. His most popular request, he said, was the first album from N.W.A. He had read that the name meant Niggaz With Attitude, and he tried to say it that way, as lazily as possible, *niggaz* with an emphasis on the end of the word rather than *niggers* with a lilt on the first syllable. Whichever way it was pronounced, Nick said, *Straight Outta Compton* was extremely popular. The profit from that album alone had brought him enough money to buy the group's second album, which had just been released. He thought it was fascinating that his best customers, not just for that particular group but also for luminaries including Big Daddy Kane and the 2 Live Crew, were sixth-grade girls who lived in my neighborhood. Maybe I could ask them for recommendations, he said, or the students from the east side, who also came to him with requests.

East San Jose, I corrected him, not the east side, and about your problem with the right way to say *nigger,* from what I've read I don't think you have any business saying that word at all. I handed him a list of requests, which he accepted with a smirk, a smirk at my old-fashioned conventions, at my lack of street cred. He brought my tapes the next day: *Straight Outta Compton, No One Can Do It Better, Rhyme Pays.* After a mute cold transaction I brought the tapes home, where they found a place of honor under my bed. And there they stayed until my family left the house, when I would pull them out and play them at full volume on my small pink tape deck. And while the music played and Almaden Valley listened, I thought about Nick's customers from the eastern part of town. I was startled but not surprised that they too were reduced to bribery and cunning to hear the music we all wanted to hear. From what I remembered of my old friends' parents—though I was already hesitant to trust my remembrances of those friends, those parents, that neighborhood—they had been just as strict as my own about their children's exposure to profanity and violence. Perhaps it was because, like my own parents, they believed that there was nothing amusing or entertaining about violence, cheap sex, self-hatred. Perhaps it was because they understood that the circumstances of being born in America placed their children closer to the reality of those things than anything that could be recorded on a tape.

SITTING NEXT TO MY BROTHER IN 1999, I wondered again about the community I'd purchased as I looked at the faces around me. They were brown and radiant and smoothed of worry. The nave swelled under the force of their voices as they sang. That morning, St. Augustine's achieved that rare moment in a Catholic mass when the flock guided the service—that moment when the church forgets the priest, forgets the proper order of things, forgets the second mortgage and the extra job, and forgets the steps outside the church.

The air tingled with the last notes of the hymn. The amazed priest eyed his congregants with a new respect. They had done well, and so he had done well. They waited for his call with pleasure. His voice was full and rich with confidence. He lifted his arms as he called them to accept the body of Christ.

The church rose, pew by pew, and moved in one line toward the altar. When it was his turn, my brother stood up beside me. He brushed off his jacket and filtered into the line shuffling up to the altar. I watched from my seat as he accepted Christ—swallowing the consecrated wafer, sipping from the jug of wine—with grave dignity. He crossed himself and then moved away.

We both noticed that the line heading up to the altar was silent and orderly. Those celebrants clasped their hands to their chests. They stared at the ground. They hummed their hymns. Only after they accepted the body of Christ did the line break down. They strolled back to their pews in couples and groups. They grinned and teased each other softly.

No one said anything to my brother.

FOR MOST OF OUR LIVES my brother and I were unable to sustain a conversation that did not dissolve into personal attacks, yelling, and punched-in walls. Such a state of affairs inevitably led to some awkward explanations as to why two people who loved each other as much as we did resorted to such forms of communication. Over the years I have stopped trying to explain something I only partially understand myself. What I can try to explain is the way I saw my brother during our teenage years: I saw a cheerful, good-natured adolescent turn into a bitter, sad adult. And I saw myself turning into an angry one.

While I was buying bootleg music and reading about the Middle Passage, shouting down my principal and hunting for the perfect T-shirt, my brother was studying Spanish and converting to Catholicism. And once he possessed language skills adequate to express what was on his mind, and the codes necessary to shape those words, my brother announced that he was changing his last name. He had no use for our father's last name, he said, with excusable if excessive histrionics, because it came from a man and a family that represented everything he wanted to avoid in his own life. Over tremendous protest the change was made—to a Spanish translation of our mother's maiden name—and my brother finished his undergraduate degree in Spanish and went on to earn a master's in Latin American Studies. And he insisted that the people around him reflect the culture and beliefs in which he was interested.

That culture and those beliefs looked strangely familiar to me: *tortas*, machismo, a house in Mexico, dreams of a first christening. *Chicanismo*. There was just one problem: The girls he dated and the men he sought for friendship treated him with overwhelming contempt. Perhaps if they had not—perhaps if the girls he dated did not dump him with the excuse of family disapproval, perhaps if his friends did not joke about him behind his back, perhaps if even the students and businessmen and gardeners he addressed in Spanish did not spit out a disgusted reply in English—perhaps if these people treated my brother differently we would not have fought. But they behaved the way they did, and my brother and I behaved the way we did. We fought. And we fought because we never bothered to look past each other's public selves. Within those public selves, my brother was battling for acceptance from a Chicano culture and I was battling for acceptance from what I believed was a black culture. We believed these two cultures were diametrically opposed, and why not? Everything we had read and seen and experienced had taught us that it was one or the other, a choice we had to make. That there was no room in the dialectic of self, of culture, for two. Only one ethnic culture can matter to you at any one time. Choose.

This is not an idle choice for people of color in America. Unlike white Americans we cannot pretend (as much as some of us would like to, as tired as we get of the discussion) to ignore this country's history of racial enmity and the hybrid cultures that formed in spite of, in resistance to, over and above that hatred. We choose because to avoid that choice would condemn us to a fate of rootlessness, of anxiety, of the terrible charge of having lost touch with our people. It is a charge that is often tacit, exuding a strange and terrible pressure. It is a charge that must not be taken lightly. I almost lost my brother over it.

The Chicanos from whom my brother sought acceptance were students, teachers, professionals—the people he met in high school and college. They were not the same people we knew as children. They were not the children who rejected me at Bret Harte. But they were still Chicano, and that was what mattered to me. Every face I saw near my brother brought back that old pain, that old distrust, and the fact that these people were rejecting my brother—who in my opinion did not deserve to be rejected for any reason—at least partially on the basis of his race made it that much worse. I always told my brother that I didn't hate Chicanos, but for a few years that was a lie. I loathed them. And every time my brother returned home in a state of despair over what one of his friends did or said to him, I panicked. I regressed into a twelve-year-old, confused and alienated, suddenly stripped of all my friends and everything I thought I knew. By the time I finished middle school I was older and stronger, more willing to assert myself, but those people were gone. The real target was missing. So it is no accident that I tended to argue with my brother immediately after he came home in states of social humiliation. His anguish frightened me. In him I saw what I might have become if I had had, at twelve years old, a thicker skin. If I had not read, at such a crucial moment, *The Autobiography of Malcolm X*. If I had fought to keep living *la lucha*, even while the people I grew up with had insisted that I must stop now; that I must find some other struggle of which to be part.

I attacked him because I was afraid that I was wrong.

I was afraid that the struggle I had chosen to be part of, the struggle as pictured on television, had no space for me. I didn't know, of course—there was no one to ask—but I had the sinking suspicion that my imagined community had nothing to do with the living, breathing realities of black lives in America. It was just conjecture. There was no way to know whether I was wrong or right. But if I was right, it would mean nothing less than the destruction of that public self I had invested all of my adolescence in constructing.

I thought I could not handle that twice.

All of this took place before I learned that if this country chose to label me as black, then I was already a living, breathing reality of black life in America; as was my brother, as we both had been from birth. All of this took place before I learned that I was a natural failure by the standards of virtually every paradigm of community currently in favor in America. All of this took place before I realized that the only thing that mattered was the private self, the self that I had neglected for so long and that I was steadily battering down in my brother out of my own fear. All of this took place before I learned that I could create and discard a thousand public selves in as many minutes with no pain. Before I learned that fear, fear of rejection, fear of failure to find acceptance somewhere—anywhere—fear of picking the wrong culture or community and being so told, left rudely adrift on the tender mercies of the American mainstream, was no excuse. Before I learned that there was no excuse. That my brother was not a receptacle for my fears, just as I should not have been for his, not something I could rail against in the hope that by hurting him, I could alleviate some of my own pain.

All of this took place before I learned that my brother was not a sacrifice to be made.

MAYBE I COULD HAVE LEARNED that lesson earlier had I listened to Guillermo, a young man who now seems all the more mystical to my mind because of my inability to trace his movements after our one and only meeting. Guillermo and my brother had been acquaintances from an early age—through school, through the neighborhood, through other friends. As they got older they stayed in touch, infrequently and in a quiet fashion. It was difficult because Guillermo left school and was rumored to be involved in gangs, while my brother had chosen the path of hard work and sober living. They had little to talk about, and both of them knew that they would not be friends for much longer. But their differences simply caused them to respect each other even more. When my brother returned home after seeing Guillermo, he always had a smile on his face. During those years my brother smiled so rarely that neither he nor anyone in our family truly wanted the relationship to end.

I called Guillermo, and just after my sixteenth birthday we met in a diner on Capital Expressway. This diner was one of the type that is now sadly facing extinction, and even at the cheerless age of sixteen I could appreciate the stark lighting, the greasy dining mats, and the red pleather booths. Of course I was dressed in my ethnic trinkets, head wrap and message T-shirt and clunky medallions, and as I walked in I confronted the types of stares that I have learned will be the tax for my passage through this world. I picked up a laminated menu, which exclusively listed foods fried in a pan, and I sat in a booth facing the expressway. From there I watched as Guillermo's car—a bottle-green Eldorado that he always drove with the top down, regardless of the season—eased into the parking lot like a crocodile slithering up the beach. Guillermo walked in a few moments later. He was magnificently dressed in a black coat that puffed around his frame like a fresh snow angel. He wore motorcycle boots and wraparound sunglasses, and when he sat down at my booth the waitress scurried to serve us as if I had not been attempting to attract her attention for the past ten minutes.

He had that effect on people. Because Guillermo was nineteen years old I came to associate that age with charm and sexual glamour. Surely he had plenty of both. It was rumored that he conditioned his hair with a paste of eggs and mayonnaise, and allowed no one but his father to trim it with cuticle scissors. The whispers were no doubt instigated out of jealousy at the result: a gleaming sheet that draped down his back, either swept back in a bandanna or plaited into a pair of black vertebrae that glimmered in the sun. It was hair that spoke for itself, just like his car. Guillermo had bought a muddy-brown drug vehicle at an auction in Oakland. Several weeks later he drove south to his cousin's garage in Rancho Cucamonga. The two men invested the greater portion of a month debating chrome trims and color gradations and leather interiors lined with white suede. They mixed and airbrushed and tinkered and trimmed, and as soon as Guillermo merged onto the northbound 101 Highway he realized he would never be able to showcase his vehicle as planned.

That was one of the hardest things I've ever had to accept, said Guillermo. I finally have the car that's haunted me for most of my life. How could I not show it? How could I hide it? This is the car that I've known as well as I know my own family. This car has been with me since I was three years old and it came to me in a vision I had after my brother returned from the First Arizona Lowrider Show at Firebird Lake in 1979.

It's hard to believe now, now that things have declined so far around here, Guillermo said, but at one time San Jose was one of the top locations for the lowriding movement. During the 1970s and 1980s King and Story roads were packed curb to curb with lowriders. As a kid I could barely walk a block in my neighborhood without seeing a shop with the capacity to transform an old abandoned car into a wondrous machine that could hop, jump, and bounce. I watched these cars with amazement because I wanted to know if the men who lifted them up to the heights of heaven could do the same for me. I once dared to ask that question of the man I admired most, my brother, who was a serious lowrider in his day. It was my brother who told me stories of suspension systems and clipped coils and grinding plates; it was my brother too who brought home the first issues of *Lowrider Magazine* when it was still a black-and-white newsletter being published here in San Jose, and it was my brother who explained to me that these cars represented not just the virtues of hard work and resourcefulness but also the pride of the entire Chicano nation.

When I asked my brother that question, Guillermo said, he was on his way to that first show in Arizona. He did not answer me for more than a week after he returned. Can you imagine how long a week is for a three-year-old? It tore me up inside. But I didn't dare pester him because he could barely speak around the tears in his eyes. Then one day he seized me and told me in a rush of the great beauty he had seen the night of that show, which took place on the Gila River Indian Reservation. The organizers had been unable to host the conference in Phoenix as planned, because the local media had sounded an alarm about what they called a convention of California gang members in their fair city. So they turned to the only sovereign people they could find: the Indians on a nearby reservation. My brother believed it was better that way, for, as he put it, the vision he had of thousands of Chicanos from Arizona, California, and Texas, gathered around Firebird Lake with the symbols of their struggle to survive and find joy in this world, was something that he would not have seen in a convention center. As he spoke I realized that my brother was answering my question. So since then I made it my mission to create the caliber of car that might have been deemed worthy to appear that night at Firebird Lake.

But I can't share my car the way I would choose, Guillermo said. I can't take it cruising, and I lock my garage every night. So far no one has managed to vandalize it, except for children who throw pebbles and small stones when I drive by, but it's a risk I've lived with ever since I brought it back. You see, I didn't realize what the reaction would be from the average *pocho* who looks at his lowrider as something to parade on Santa Clara Street. They lack what they call the time and resources but what I call the simple imagination to make their own cars look like the visions that we have in our dreams, and so they'd want to destroy mine. It's a danger I live with gladly, every moment of every day, even while sitting in a diner with such fine company. Even as we are drinking this coffee I'm listening to the noises outside: the pounding of tires on the highway, the footsteps on the pavement leading up to the door, the slam of car doors. If I stop listening I might miss something. And all it takes is a moment. He paused and smiled broadly, and because he mentioned the word *pocho* I felt a need to open up the crucial subject of conversation.

I was hoping to talk to you about my brother, I said.

Really, he said.

Yes. I know that you might think it's strange since you don't know him very well anymore, but I know him even less than you do. And surely you can't find this request any stranger than getting a phone call from me, someone you've never properly met, with a demand for a meeting.

All kinds of people call me and want to talk, said Guillermo. People I've met. People I haven't met. I didn't find it strange at all.

Outside, the sun was slowly shifting across the highway. Thin bands of shade settled on Guillermo's face, and as he stared at me the irises of his eyes deepened and darkened. It was said that the gang with which he ran had splintered from the Norteños on important policy matters, and because this group had broken away, they had more enemies than any other gang in town. And yet they thrived, it was said, because of their exercise of the policies that until this time the Norteños had declined to practice: breaking their enemies through harm to their children, trafficking in the drugs that sold in wealthier parts of town, following through on all their threats. These were the rumors about Guillermo. They were probably spread by the same people who whispered about eggs and mayonaise, but still I felt the danger of this man, even if it was just the danger of wanting him to touch me, and this danger became more palpable with every moment I tried to rush through a conversation that could have proved far more valuable to all parties involved.

I don't know what you and my brother talk about, I said. I'm sure he doesn't talk to you about the things that hurt him, that keep him from sleeping, that make him scream and yell and tear out of the house at night in an unseeing rage. I'm sure he doesn't share those things and neither do you. You're men. But I need to share something with you about my brother's life that bothers me, and please don't think less of him because of it. It's quite simple and it could happen to anyone, really. With the exception of you, nearly everyone my brother calls a friend treats him badly. I know you don't know these people.

What, are they Chicano? said Guillermo. Is that why you called me? Did you think I could explain their behavior? Unlock the mystery?

Look, I know how angry I'd be if someone asked me to do that for black people, I said. And that's not exactly my question. So please don't be offended—

Guillermo chuckled and motioned to the waitress. She grabbed the plastic handle of a coffeepot and rushed over. She poured him another cup and, after many breathless inquiries, returned to her post behind the long Formica counter. I had long since abandoned hope of an exhibition of her interest in my needs, and so I waited until the steam had cleared from Guillermo's face before I leaned over the table and repeated that I knew I would be offended at the same question. I didn't expect him to explain the behavior of my brother's friends, but maybe he had some thoughts on my brother's behavior.

He had lots of thoughts on my brother's behavior, he said, and while he didn't pretend to have anything in common with the group with which my brother ran, he had a guess about why they acted the way they did. For example, he would place a wager that some of them did not speak Spanish. Or maybe they did, but they didn't speak it well, and this had been a source of embarrassment to their families on the annual trip to Guadalajara—was I maybe understanding what he was trying to say? I was not, and he pointed out to me that maybe it had been okay with these friends that they did not speak Spanish, and maybe it had even been okay with their families while they were on my brother's side of the border, but when they were faced with this brother of mine, this *negrono*, who not only spoke their language but knew their history and studied their books and practiced their religion and tried just a little bit too hard to have everything they thought belonged to them—was I maybe now understanding what he was trying to say?

I was and he settled back into the booth with his relief, his coffee cup, his stare. He was glad I understood, he said, and perhaps now I could share something about my life with him. I would be offended if someone posed the same question to me about black people, so he would ask me a different question. He wondered how many black people I actually knew.

IT WAS A QUESTION I could have, and should have, answered then, because it's obvious to me now that Guillermo already knew the answer. He also knew that the answer would make me break. He knew this, and that is why I would not answer. Because I could not, would not chuckle along as he burst into irrepressible laughter. Because I could not stomach another intrusion from the waitress with the plastic-handled coffeepot, running over to soothe Guillermo's laughter-induced coughing. Because I could not sob in front of him. Because I could not bear his attempts to soothe me, his shaky pats on my hand, his murmuring concern about why I was weeping. Because I knew, as he did, that all of this would happen as soon as I admitted that my brother was not alone in trying too hard, as soon as I tried to talk about the number of black people I knew.

I could have saved myself four more years of painful self-delusion if I had just answered Guillermo's question.

. . .

MY BROTHER STRODE BACK to our pew and smiled at me. The smile was tentative, but his mood was lighter. Mass was almost over and I had behaved well. He had expected the worst, but with the exception of a few glances askance, a few grumbles about my dress from the older women in the next pew, things went smoothly. I was animated and alert. I grinned back at my brother. His face cleared. He dropped his hand to my shoulder.

The priest sang to the church, raising the book above his head. His face, too, was clear. His mass went as well as my brother's. Often the flock breaks down after taking communion. People duck out for other Sunday commitments. Babies begin to fret. From the parking lot an announcement blares about someone's double parking. The remaining flock stirs and becomes restless. Children giggle and play in the aisles. Couples disappear in the nook of a statue for a kiss. Older members shuffle in the pews. The calm of church is broken by coughing and sneezing and all those other noises of agitation and annoyance and gross human need.

But on that August morning there was none of that. No intrusion of the people's crasser desires, the pressures of Los Angeles, or even the beggars on the steps. The parish offered the full attention of their bright brown faces.

My brother's hand rested on my shoulder as he led me through the prayer and benediction like a sympathetic tour guide. Hold hands, he whispered. Frantically I groped for the hand of the woman next to me. Her lips soured, but she placed her limp hand in mine. I hoisted our strange appendage in the air and we waited for the moment to give our signs of peace.

IN THE MOMENT before our peace I thought back to the year before.

I was in San Jose for the Christmas holidays, and I was afflicted with a familiar sense of restlessness and oblique anxiety. It was the same sort of affliction that always debilitates me shortly before I make unfortunate life decisions. So I was cautious. I slept when I could. I worked steadily but not to excess. I refused to see anyone except a few dear friends. I ate regular balanced meals and only occasionally took controlled substances. I paced the house. I rarely went out.

And then one afternoon when the sky was leaden and the wind was hot and dry and my family was irritable and the phone would not stop ringing I stood up and I left. There were keys on the kitchen table and I grabbed them; I climbed in a car and I began to drive at a speed too reckless for Almaden Valley. The highway numbers increased along with my speedometer: 85 South, 87 North, 680 East. By the time I turned off on Capital Expressway my screeching tires were loud enough to frighten me. I slowed down for the turn onto Alum Rock Boulevard and watched the side streets fan out before me like a peacock's tail. Even now I can close my eyes and see those streets; and down those streets I can see Alum Rock Park, where as a young child I hid among mountainous rocks and sandboxes and avoided the men who, as my mother informed me, were inhaling things that made them ravenous for the flesh of little girls; I can see the Capitol flea market, where it is still possible to buy tortillas with lard as you stroll through aisles of gilt picture frames and worn cowboy boots and sun-beaten field hats; I can see Andrew Hill High School, which has twice been placed on the list of the city's potential school failures and might have been my alma mater had things been different. In my mother's mustard-yellow 1983 Volvo I made the turn off of Flint Street onto Gila Drive and pulled up to the curb in front of our old house. It still had its modest bungalow design, its neat green lawn, its calla lilies blooming outside my bedroom window. Once yellow, the house is now painted a tasteful shade of gray, and since we left it has passed into the hands of Vietnamese immigrants and Filipino missionaries, but when I pulled up to the door I saw no one but a pair of young Chi-canos. They stood on the sidewalk and watched me switch off the ignition and activate the automatic door locks. They were maybe fif-teen years old, and despite their loose-fitting clothes I could see that neither of them weighed more than one hundred and ten pounds. Nonetheless they stared at me with a shrewd feline grace and I re-membered that age and build may count for nothing in delicate situa-tions. One of them was wearing a red T-shirt, something I dared not do when I lived in this house.

They kept up their silent, watchful stares as I introduced myself and told them that I was visiting my old house. My family moved to Almaden years ago, I said, and my brother and I still miss this place.

My name's Javier, said the one wearing red. My family used to live down the street, close to Melvin the car mechanic, if you remember him. Now we live five blocks away and I walk back and forth to Andrew Hill High School. It's gotten to the point where my family can't pay for both our house and our car, and I'm sure we'll move soon. To Hollister, or to Stockton, or someplace where people drive three hours a day to get to real jobs. Because no one can afford to live even here anymore without a college degree and a computer job. But you've seen that on your side of town for a long time, haven't you.

You could say that, I said. Do you know what happened to the other people who used to live on this street?

Most of them have moved on, Javier said.

The black folks, too? I said.

Ah, he said. If you're looking for the black people who used to live here, I'm sorry to tell you that there aren't many left. Ingrid's family has long since left for cheaper pastures and I haven't seen Paula in years. My guess is that it's only a matter of time until the men in white coats drag out her naked screaming body while a police squad cordons off the street to retrieve the bags of prescription pills and white powder. But that time hasn't come yet, and until then all I can say is that she's the last on this street. The rest have left, and we will be the next to go.

WHEN THE MASS ENDED and the church turned to go in peace, the beggars were off the steps. The nurse had wheeled them into position near the side entrance, and the congregation flooded the threshold with relief. Now the parishioners could leave St. Augustine's and their duty to Christ without confronting despair. The beggars still called out for alms; their Styrofoam cups still tocked out an unending keen, but their power was slight. Mass was over. Sin had been absolved. It was an August morning in Los Angeles, and the world was shiny new. There was no room for poverty, for wretchedness.

And so we left, to deal with the headaches of life after Christ, with the houses in Echo Park, the car-repair bills, the children. A few worshippers lingered in the parking lot—cousins greeted each other, children scruffed their whites with a game of tag—and my brother spotted two familiar faces.

David and Terry, he said with another grab of my shoulder. He introduced me in Spanish. I smiled and made nice, and he let me go. I drifted away and watched as they conversed in that language that still to me sounds like a forbidden tongue. I shivered.

The young man was slender and wore glasses. His hair rested on his forehead in two thickly oiled crumpets. He did not know what to do with his hands. They jumped across his thighs, folded over his chest, fidgeted, groped for his girlfriend's hand. But the rest of his body was calm, and he engaged my brother with slow nods and thoughtful responses. My brother responded with long stories of good times. They laughed. Their eyes danced.

The girlfriend was quieter. She did not know my brother very well, and she did not know me at all, so she played shy. When her boyfriend's hand stopped dancing, she clung to that. With her other hand she clutched her purse tight, and she looked no one in the eye. But she kept up with the conversation, laughed at the appropriate moments. Twice she ventured a comment of her own, and my brother turned to her with interested eyes, nodding, drawing her in.

He was more comfortable with them than he was with me.

He had finally found a few people who appreciated him for who he is, which is the best any of us can hope for, and perhaps the reason we did not fight that week was not just because I was incapacitated by heartbreak but also because he had reaped the rewards of asserting himself over all of it—the din of the American mainstream, the Chicanos who rejected him, me and my own pain. He found a few friends who knew what he had always known: that it is only right and proper to take pride in the culture in which you grew up, even if it makes people afraid, even if it makes them question their reflexive beliefs, and especially if it makes them remember that there are things to fight for and that an exclusive claim on struggle in America is not one of them. I accepted this second lesson with less shock than I would have expected. I felt it with a slight shake, as if a breeze had passed. And I wished, once again, for a shawl.

CHAPTER TWO

THIS IS A STORY I've told before.

I published my first piece of writing at the age of sixteen, an article for *West*, the Sunday magazine of the *San Jose Mercury News*. When I first approached the editors there, I didn't have an article or even an idea for an article. What I had was a grievance. Being sixteen years old, I had plenty of them, but I thought this one was special, and while I know now that it wasn't, they were kind enough to listen. The sum of my grievance was this: I was a conscious black woman in a white world. (My definitions of consciousness and blackness and whiteness would prove less resilient later, but when I was sixteen, they were sheathed in steel.)

I was aggrieved at having grown up in San Jose, a city that had been steadily losing its small black population to the skyrocketing property costs and mass gentrification wrought by a technology boom. I was aggrieved by the actions of my parents, who had moved us from our childhood neighborhood, where the schools were lacking but a polyglot ethnic mix gave us some aspirations to what I thought of as authenticity, to Almaden Valley, where for years we were the only people of any color in the neighborhood. I attended an all-girls Catholic high school with an average of three black students per grade level.

These circumstances alone offered me any number of offensive experiences to choose from. (And I was on the lookout.) The one I alighted on with particular fervor was what I judged to be the attitude of my school toward my attempts to inject a black presence into the curriculum. For two and a half years they had thwarted me. By *they* I meant the school's staff, administration, and students, but I also meant a larger and more overarching force that I could feel but not articulate. I meant the blind but not benign eye that America turns to race. I meant the pointed way in which the people of my neighborhood spoke of plummeting property values and bad influences and cultural differences when they spoke of busing or crime or drugs. I meant the refusal of my school, my neighbors, my city, and of course—since I am talking about America and, more to the point, California—my television and newspaper and movie screen to speak frankly about what had never really faded from their minds.

At my school this refusal took simple forms. The administration's approach consisted of a series of evasions. I could not form a black student union or request an assembly for Black History Month or even put up my own posters in the hallways. The reasoning for rejecting the student union was that it bordered on a separatist enterprise and students who weren't black might feel excluded. Regarding Black History Month, it was a question of fairness: If something was done for Black History Month, then something had to be done for every culture, and did I know how many different cultures were in America? Well. There just weren't enough months in the year.

Given the peculiar power imbalance between students and administrators, I could argue only so long with their reasoning; but I could, and did, in the article, point out that something in this approach left me feeling unacknowledged. To further my argument, I re-created an exchange that had taken place two years before, between myself and my freshman-year history teacher. Lecturing on slavery, the teacher explained that in comparison with slavery in the Caribbean, slavery in America wasn't that bad. Something about her statement struck me as terribly, hauntingly wrong, but I could not speak up for various reasons, mostly because I had no concrete proof to the contrary. (I did not yet understand that it is impossible to quantify, reduce, or compare dehumanizing experiences of any sort.) Instead I stayed after class to speak to her, an encounter I always recall with shame, because I broke down in tears and was unable to speak or eat for the rest of the day. She pulled up a chair, and I stammered out my request: Might it be possible for us to talk more about black American history in class, and to talk about black people other than as slaves? She replied that she was doing the best she could with the time she had, and that I needed to understand that there were lots of things in the curriculum to cover. It was at this point that I disgusted myself by coming to pieces, and she pursed her lips and patted my arm.

Although I discussed all these incidents in the *West* article, ultimately the piece became more amorphous than the story of confrontation between Me and Racism. I spoke of my failure to find a black community or any community at all, my struggle to figure out what, if anything, it meant to be black—I spoke a sweet, awkward story about searching for what we have come to call identity. The piece ran in full color with an author photograph and a modest byline indicating only that I was a high school junior in San Jose. I scrupulously avoided naming my school and my teachers in an effort to respect their privacy. My effort was completely useless.

The article was published on a Sunday. The next Tuesday I stood outside the principal's office, listening to a screaming match between the principal, one of my editors, and my mother. On Wednesday I stood inside the classroom of my freshman-year history teacher, studying the one hundred or so student signatures on a petition in support of the school, the history teacher, and punishment for the author of a recent piece that accused the school of racism. On Friday I stood in the police station, registering both an unsigned threat I had received in the mail and a report about my car, which had been battered with a blunt object while I was in class. And on the Sunday following, I stood in my local bookstore with the newspaper and read a letter to the editor of *West* magazine, signed by a student at my school, that politely disagreed with my article, claiming that her experience had been wonderfully multicultural, thanks to the school's numerous efforts to further diversity.

This is the story I have told before, many times before. I have told it at cocktail receptions and dinner parties, at scholarship interviews and in my college-application essay. And every time I have told it, it has won me respect and admiration. It is that rare tale that appeals to every audience. Some people enjoy it because they think they can compare favorably to the villains; they believe they would have behaved with more grace and maturity in the same situation, and it feels good to believe that. Others enjoy it because it reinforces their a priori beliefs about white communities in Almaden Valley, in California, in America. Some people like it quite simply because it is a classic underdog story with a Hollywood ending: I struggled on at that school for another year and a half, struggled through the silent hostility, and I graduated in a shower of scholarships and awards, to become the school's first alumna accepted to Harvard. The college admissions officers, I have imagined, were part of the last group, seeing a place for themselves in the Hollywood narrative and acting accordingly.

For a few years, I too saw a place for myself in that narrative. I liked sharing it with people. I felt, and still feel, that it is an important story to share: the type of quintessentially American story that reveals our serious subterranean fears about power and access and, of course, about race. I also liked to share it because I look good in it: powerful and provocative and assertive, capable of bringing an entire school to drastic measures and ultimately rising above their small minds. I look a lot less confused, angry, and terrified than I was.

But I don't get much pleasure out of sharing this story anymore. I don't like it now for precisely the same reason that I used to like it years ago: I look powerful and provocative and assertive, rather than the way I truly felt at the time. I don't like it now because people tend to extrapolate from the narrative a vision of who I am (bold, out-spoken, righteous) that has only rarely had any similarity to the way I deal with racism. In real life, as opposed to on the page, I am, like many people of color, struck dumb when confronted with racism. I am inarticulate on the best of days; in the face of the nasty joke, the clerk sniffing behind me as I move around the store, the teacher who can't be bothered to speak reasonably about slavery, I am helpless to piece together a coherent response. I sob, stammer, fume wordlessly, or in some other humiliating fashion miss my chance to speak up. This is the way I deal with life, not just racism, and it has become one of the primary reasons that I hide behind a pen.

But the fact remains that when people hear this story, they fail to understand that if I felt anything at all during that bewildering week and the year and a half to come, it wasn't rebelliousness or satisfaction or even anger. It was conflict and fright, two emotions that do not jibe, that simply do not fit in with a narrative that ends in triumph. These feelings have no place in a narrative that appeals to so many people, a narrative that has helped me earn so many free drinks and scholarships, a narrative that made the admissions boards at every college to which I applied stand up and applaud. (In the acceptance package I received from Brown University, for example, there was a page of glowing comments about this story.) In short, these are feelings that have no place in an identity narrative, and when I insist on including them they spoil the whole story.

I would like to take a moment to spoil this story. I should first explain how I came to be at that all-girls Catholic school. I come from a family whose basal instrument in its fight for success and dignity has been education. The major reason that we moved from east San Jose to Almaden Valley as soon as we were economically stable was that the public schools in Almaden had the best rankings in the city. Most of the children who went to Almaden's public schools went on to college; their test scores on the state exams were exemplary. The schools still had art and music classes; physical education was mandatory, not a wistful thought. My parents wanted their children to benefit from these resources, so they moved into the school district, at great financial strain to themselves, until an enormous real-estate boom in the Bay Area kindled by an illusionary decade of economic growth offered my parents and countless other families who were house-rich and cash-poor the luxury of an equity cushion. My parents believed that the sacrifices they were making for their children's education in California's better public schools would be amply recompensed, just as the sacrifices their own parents made had been. One after the other my brother and I went to Bret Harte Middle School. And one after the other my parents realized that we would have to look elsewhere for our education.

I can speak only of my own experience at Bret Harte, and of it I can say only that its nuances lie beyond my capacity for understanding. I do not know how I came to lose my enthusiasm there. At no point in my life have my parents ever encouraged me to take my academics lightly; at no point have I ever abandoned my books, my fascination with history, my ability to focus on an intellectual task to the point of complete absorption. But while I was at Bret Harte I lost my ability to perform academically, and as soon as I was out of that environment I realized that I was not the only one at fault. The climate at Bret Harte was not receptive to my success. There were real racists at that school, like the administrator who took one look at me and refused to test me for the gifted and talented program. I remember a teacher who would not give me good grades no matter what kind of work I turned in—I came home in tears more than once when she had returned my reports with demerits so opaque and arbitrary that even she could not explain them. Another teacher told my parents he believed it was a waste of time to teach me grammar and spelling, and he bore this out in class, although mercifully he did not repeat his comment to me. These were the educators I had to contend with at Bret Harte. These were people with real problems, and most of the other teachers and administrators were too dispirited from the conditions of working in a California public school to offer me any support or even, with the exception of my beloved eighth-grade history teacher, Stafford Baham, to notice me at all.

And I was equipping myself to fight this with the black militancy I learned from books; I was weaponless, in other words. I might have been able to identify my challenge had it come in the form of the public insults and physical attacks I had been trained to look for by Malcolm, Eldridge et al., but there was little in those books about quiet, contemporary racism with a smile. So I continued to read them during class and wondered, dimly, why school suddenly held so little interest for me. I was too naïve to recognize what was right in front of me and too untrained to shape it into words even if I had recognized it. My academic capacity might have continued to deteriorate all through high school had not my parents been far savvier than I was. They are public school teachers themselves, and they have seen too much of the results from low expectations and administrative neglect in their own lives. They put aside their need for new cars and took on extra jobs during the summer, and they took my brother and me out of the public education system. What they heard—from other teachers who had faced the same problems—

was that the best private schools in San Jose were Catholic, and that is why they sent us there.

By the time I entered Presentation High School I had lived in Almaden Valley for more than three years. My parents separated for the last time when I was eleven, and reconciled when I was thirteen; since then they have lived together in a state of tenuous acceptance and shocking stability in the large family house in Almaden. Both of them were earning more money than I could ever remember us having; their careers seemed to be following that familiar trajectory of growth, which surprised no one except themselves. Tentatively, my family began to assume the concerns and the anxieties of the upper middle class.

For me, these concerns and anxieties came in the form of an unstoppable drive for academic achievement. I want to be cautious in my description here; achievement is not, nor should it be, solely the interest of the affluent. But the upper middle class does have an unhealthy obsession with a specific sort of academic and monetary competition, mostly because it seems to bolster identities that are shaky in the best of times.

And part of my newfound drive came from the school itself. Whatever its failings, Presentation offered me the opportunity to thrive. My teachers were passionate about their subjects and stuck to a fair grading policy. The administrators tested everyone to gauge our fitness for advanced courses. My teachers pushed me and made it clear that anything less than my best effort would be unacceptable, and it worked. I learned to love academics again, and I became my own best coach. The other students were more girls from Almaden, and I found it difficult to get along with girls in general and girls from Almaden in particular; but I understood the importance of acting innocuous and insincere now, another sign of how well my family had settled into our neighborhood. I refused to acknowledge that I was comfortable in Almaden. I was still seething at my parents for moving and disrupting any claim I might have had to the authenticity of struggle.

All of this was built into the conflict I felt about my article. I knew that Presentation had offered me my greatest opening for academic merit. I knew that I was preoccupied with achievement, and that publishing a long story in the Sunday magazine of a major newspaper is no small achievement for a sixteen-year-old. This led to the fright: I was afraid of what my school might do to me, but I was also afraid of what I had done to *it,* and why. Eventually I came to believe that the ire I had unleashed was based on not just my high school's errors but also the inexcusable actions of the authorities at my middle school. I had had no opportunity to punish Bret Harte, and I was furious that the only way for me to overcome that situation had been to leave for private education—an option, I fully realized even at sixteen, that was not open to many families. So I used my anger from that experience in lashing out at the place that came next.

And for what cause? Surely, for the cause of my own shaky identity as someone who was down with the struggle, and surely out of anguish and humiliation at the injustices I really had suffered, and surely because publishing a long story in the Sunday magazine of a major newspaper is no small achievement for a sixteen-year-old.

Now I have come clean and ruined a story that formed a critical part of who I once presented myself to be. There are a lot of identity narratives that would be spoiled if their narrators came clean. When I talk about identity narratives, I am speaking of the accounts that tend to come from young people my age, stories written or spoken for competition in the races that upper-middle-class adults and their children are always running. I am speaking of many of the narratives designed for college entrance and scholarship panels and grant interviews. I am speaking of the narratives whose purpose is the composition itself.

Certainly the idea of identity creation for profit's sake is not a new one, or even one that should cause alarm. We all wish to impress friends and strangers, to get free drinks, to perform well during the job interview. We have all benefited from use of the brave face in times of hardship, the cheerful persona for periods of depression, the compassionate act in the face of another's loss. These are the lies that sustain families and societies; these faces constitute what we have come to call, in some particularly well-practiced people, discretion.

The trouble arises when we start believing in our creations and putting them up for sale. And what I see among that group of young people for whom life is an endless series of high-stakes competitions is a cynical belief that the purpose of identity narratives is to impress others, not to define one's own morals, values, or behavior. I have occasionally been guilty of this belief myself, although I cannot agree with it. But perhaps because I grew up in Silicon Valley and went to an ambitious high school and then to an even more ambitious college, I do possess an understanding of how it can consume you.

Three years after the *West* article was published, I received a phone call from Lila, my best (and usually only) friend in high school. It was February in Cambridge, and I huddled in my sophomore-year dorm room, wrapped in a mille-feuille of blankets. Outside, the ground was awash with mud and sludge, the airless sky tingled with the promise of snow. I did not want to stand up for that phone call. In my quest to put three thousand miles and, I hoped, at least that many worlds between myself and San Jose, I hadn't anticipated the less glamorous side of East Coast winters. My room was well heated, but I was always cold, even hours after I had come indoors. After the first snowball fights I burrowed in my room for four months, barely moving, loath to budge for meals or classes or even a phone call across the room.

But I gathered my layers around me and waddled to the phone. I was surprised and pleased to hear from Lila; our phone conversations had grown rare since I left for college. We were inseparable in high school. She was the strange one, with a rotating palette of hair color and drug paraphernalia in her locker, and I was the sullen one, studying so hard that I seemed to carry a grudge against my lessons. What bound us together, apart from a refined contempt for our surroundings, was a common hunger for more than what we sensed was on offer from any given situation. Together we tried everything we could think of to find the mysteries that were, we were sure, lurking behind the stymied surface of our lives: drugs, travel, shopping, starvation, dangerous men. As soon as we graduated it became clear that our temperaments were drastically different. Her desires were inchoate; she unleashed her remarkable intelligence on personal relationships and social spheres; she enjoyed being liked and admired. I fixate on goals and action and movement with the fervor of the possessed; I prefer to be disliked, or at least underestimated, if it helps me perform the task at hand. I suppose it was natural for us to grow apart, though I still feel the loss keenly. There was also the matter of geographic distance: She moved to London within six months of our graduation. But she returned to San Jose for frequent visits, and in fact, she had just come home (meaning London—it was amazing how quick we were then to claim another place, any place other than San Jose) from California, she said. The trip had been miserable as usual, and she felt no need to recap the reasons why we both had left. But, she said, she did learn an interesting story, and the purpose of her call was to share it with me. During her visit she had haunted the local shopping mall, and it was there that she ran into Alice. In high school Alice had associated herself with the highest-achieving students in our class and had made it clear, both before and after the *West* article, that she thought very little of me. It was Alice who told Lila this story.

I didn't wish to hear it. Mention of the girl's name brought back everything I was running from: the conflict, the fright, the pain of my last years in high school. But Lila insisted on continuing, explaining that the story had to do with my article—*that* article—and that it was, moreover, an interesting story. When she said this, I truly had no desire to hear it, since unlike the rest of San Jose I was ready to let *that* article go. Even three years on, I was unable to enter a public space in San Jose without suffering a confrontation with someone over *that* article, usually a middle-aged man whose daughters had attended my school. I no longer enjoyed the notoriety, and the novelty of recognition had worn thin. But Lila was on the phone, Lila, whom I had looked up to so much during high school and whose existence had always seemed so much more charmed than my own. I always, sometimes foolishly, hungered after every word she said. And what she said on that cold February day was that Alice was suffering pangs of conscience. So she offered me this confession, said Lila, and I cannot believe she did not intend me to share it with you. Alice was ashamed of her friends' behavior during the week after my article was published. Like many students, this group of girls met to gossip about the piece; like many students, they speculated about what the administration would do to me, taking for granted, of course, that punishment was the proper response. But unlike other students, these girls had a very personal reaction to the controversy, out of which came the petition posted in my freshman history teacher's classroom.

I've since spent some time considering what might have motivated these girls to respond in such a way. I understand that they were, first and foremost, children of Almaden Valley. They seemed to believe wholeheartedly in the values of Silicon Valley in general and Almaden Valley in particular: all-consuming work and constant competition, esurience and solipsism, and that all of these values were burnished to a fine shine with a gloss of concern for human progress. *Progress* was one of the lofty words running rampant in the valley at that time. The girls at my school looked at themselves and their neighborhood and found no reason to doubt the values. And for an overachieving high school student there can be no greater goal than gaining entrance to the best colleges in the nation.

You might understand what it meant for these girls to spend their every waking moment focused on the pursuit of college acceptances if you understand their average day:

6:30: wake up

7:15–11:40: classes

11:40–12:05: lunchtime Debate Team meeting

12:07–12:20: lunchtime Science Club meeting

12:25–2:10: classes

2:15–3:15: Student Council meeting

3:30–5:30: community service

5:30–8:00: basketball practice (or dance lessons)

8:30–12:30: homework and studying

12:45: bedtime

I can use this schedule as an example because it mirrored my own during these years. I can also say from experience that such a rigid system of control has a tendency to spill over into other life choices, such as diet or association. This lifestyle is debilitating, of course, and for many years I believed it was only because of the exhaustion factor, but now I wonder if what is truly exhausting about it is that it encourages a slavish devotion to authority.

Did these girls feel undirected and unspoken resentment at the state of affairs, as I occasionally did? And since I chose not to pick my friends from the ranks of the high-achieving, I wondered, did their shared goals affect their friendships? Did they conclude that college entrance was a race to be run against everyone, including one another? Did they remind each other of the oblique anxiety and animosity with which they all battled every day?

For example, the girl from whom Lila heard part of this story was struggling a bit more than her friends; she earned slightly lower grades and participated in fewer leadership activities; she brought a piece of chocolate cake to this meeting and ate it while the other girls pretended not to watch; she despised both me and her friends with equal force but could only express her feelings for me. I believe that it was because of these things—the lower grades and the fewer activities and especially the chocolate cake—that she articulated the desires of the group by suggesting a petition. And then you can understand that it was because of those same things that she later felt guilty, and decided to confess to the one person who would certainly tell me.

At least that is how I understand it now. I lived this life, and had this schedule, for long enough to recognize what was reflecting off of these girls' faces every time we smiled at each other in the hall. I chose to have no friends—except for Lila, who was wholly uninterested in this sort of tactical planning—rather than to compete with the people from whom I might want emotional support later. This was my strategy, and I thought that it might keep me safe. I didn't realize that it existed mainly in the confines of my own imagination. They thought you'd betrayed them, said Lila. That came up again and again at their meeting, and it must have been the word lurking beneath the surface of their petition and those letters to the editor. When Alice told me this I tried to imagine those letters to the editor, none of which were printed and so will remain lost to memory: what could they have written? That they felt betrayed by you? That they believed you were one of their own? You were an honorary member, too brooding and angry for full-fledged participation but a junior partner, because of your grades and your activities and the jokes you cracked about life without food or sleep. And you did them harm, because you knew this was a race, and races have rules, and you deliberately broke them. You pulled an illegal move to set yourself apart from the pack, and you undermined their chances.

I interrupted Lila to ask if Alice was being serious. C'mon, I said, she and her friends didn't believe that I had published that article for the purpose of bettering my odds in the college sweepstakes. And certainly, I said, they can't think that anything I did had even the slightest effect on their own odds.

Why not? said Lila. It makes sense. Your article reflects poorly on the school, the school gets a bad reputation, everyone's affected. And so they thought maybe the petition would be a corrective measure— although you must be happy to know that in the end it only made for a better story from your side.

I turned toward my window in Cambridge, where outside the snow had started falling. I had no way of knowing this from my room; the light was feeble, the windowpanes were greasy, and the gray-marble sky was just as restless as it had been all day. When I moved to Cambridge, the first thing I learned about snow was that when it begins to fall—those first snowflakes, tiny as dust motes, not white but the color of dinge—it is impossible to see or feel or taste. The only way to know the snow has begun is to listen. A full, profound silence, thick with the double-edged possibility of angels and blizzards, sinks in right before the first of the snow. It is eerie and intuitive and if a breeze cuts across this silence it feels like the same breeze that rattles windowpanes and shatters nerves in the foehn wind of the Southern California desert. The silence lasts just moments, and I had heard the last of it with the end of Lila's sentence, but I turned now to listen for it again.

I was listening to that silence as if it could tell me something that Lila could not—Lila, who had been kind enough to support me during that difficult time and was now calling for my attention on the other end of the phone line. For days to come I did nothing but listen for that silence at my window. I listened for it long after it had disappeared into the howls and the wind and the patter—the snow in hard white bullets now—that attends a storm. I listened at my window, knowing full well that the silence had disappeared as soon as I heard it, and I pieced together narratives. I pieced together these girls' stories, both the one I had, in their eyes, ruined and the one that eventually came to replace it. Clean hard moments bobbed to the surface of my memory and I sat by my window in Cambridge, watching a storm, eating smuggled crackers from the dining hall, listening to silence and the workings of my own mind. I laughed at myself and at how oblivous I had been. I had never realized I was considered welcome in the company of those girls at all, and I certainly had not realized they considered my actions treacherous. I knew, of course, that they snubbed me; I knew that our relations deteriorated after my article was published. By the spring semester of our senior year all civility had vanished. But I had never questioned why. Granted, I had other things on my mind at the time. There were, as always, the classes and activities and studying, but there were also the college applications and standardized tests and the pressures that come from walking down halls every day to be met with averted eyes. All those things drove me further into an inwardness I have carried since birth, an inwardness that at that time was growing increasingly self-destructive. I barely noticed anyone around me senior year, and I certainly didn't pay attention to the minute shifts in power and strategic alliance that form the atmosphere of an all-girls high school. But there was a moment in which I noticed how those girls' feelings toward me had irrevocably crystallized.

This happened during the waning days of our senior year in high school, shortly after college decisions were due. I had decided to go to Harvard, and though I would have preferred to keep the news to myself, word got out rather quickly. (The leak was probably my own mother, who turned up at the principal's office with a copy of my acceptance letter and a big grin.) There was a change in the way people spoke to me after this—in the fact that they spoke at all—but I remained aloof, drifting through the halls in my bleary fog. In fact, it was while drifting through the halls, which were deserted after school, that I heard a girl sobbing. I paused, at first out of the tentativeness that comes with interrupting a breakdown, and then because she started to yell. She was sobbing and yelling at her boyfriend, and the subject of her explosion was me. I slipped behind a row of lockers and considered the voice. Sara was by far one of the most ambitious girls in our class. She was friends with Alice and had participated in the meeting that led to the petition, although I didn't know this at the time. What I did know was that she exerted an influence over her group of friends, and occasionally the school's staff and administration, that was unmatched by any other student. Despite this, she was upset—dreadfully upset—that I was going to Harvard. She didn't deserve to get in, Sara sobbed. She didn't deserve to get in. None of *us* got in. *None* of us. She only got in because she's black, and because she got to write an essay that the school is racist. Comforting murmurs, presumably from her boyfriend, followed this declaration, and Sara drew in several long, shaky breaths. Then she burst into tears again. She didn't even take honors chemistry, she sobbed. And now she's being *smug* about the whole thing.

It had not been my intention to be smug, but I turned away from the row of lockers with a slight smirk on my face, and I'm pleased to report that it remained there until I walked across the makeshift auditorium stage on my graduation day. I felt smug after hearing Sara in the hallway, but not because I was going to Harvard and she wasn't. I felt smug because I was leaving Silicon Valley and Almaden, and because I was going to a place where I believed I would be surrounded by like-minded people: people who were bright enough, and confident enough, to play by a higher standard. I believed that Harvard would encourage people of merit, not people of machination. I believed that I would hear no identity narratives there, and tell none of my own, because they would no longer be a necessary form of social interaction.

I don't know how I came by this way of thinking. At any rate, I soon learned that matters at Harvard worked to the contrary. It was an agonizing disappointment. Among the casualties of this realization was my friend Spencer.

I met Spencer during my first week on campus. First-year students have more than a week to unpack their belongings and find their bearings unmolested before the upperclassmen return for classes. During this time there are a few upperclassmen on campus, of course: dorm cleaning-crew workers, docents, and leaders of some of the student organizations. Spencer fell within the last group. He returned early to publicize his community-service project to the new class. I met him at some dimly lit, zombie-ish activity fair. I wandered into his table, punch-drunk with information, and he watched me read his flyer uncomprehendingly at least three times before he reached out, very gently, and peeled it out of my hands. I blinked and looked up at him. His eyes were arctic blue and his cheeks were china white. Those cheeks were so translucent that they pulsed pink in the cold. He smiled at me.

We could talk about it, he said. He glanced at the flyer he had removed from the assault of my glazed eyes. He smiled again, wider this time. We could talk, he said. It doesn't have to hurt.

Spencer was two years older than me. When we met, he was already thoroughly indoctrinated in the mores of life on campus. He knew all the substrata and all the politics of student life; he moved with ease, charm, and no small amount of humor among them all. With the exception of Guillermo, I had never met anyone so comfortable with himself. It was a mesmerizing thing to watch him stride through the Yard with his lacrosse stick, which I first mistook for a butterfly net. In San Jose there is little idea of what lacrosse means. There is little idea of what butterfly hunting means either. I hid my ignorance when he told me, in a rush, that he played lacrosse for pure enjoyment of the game and that he held most lacrosse players in complete contempt—a wonderful game played by the silliest people, he said. He assumed, wrongly, that I understood the sociopolitical implications of lacrosse, and I did not want to disabuse him of the notion.

At first I thought Spencer's sense of ease had to do with his worldliness. He talked about Aspen and Sun Valley (Garish, but that's to be expected, he said; I keep to myself and concentrate on the snow) and Portofino and Paris, and he talked about these places casually, without a trace of ostentation or desperation, which let me know that there had been more places in the past and there would be more in the future. At first I did not think to connect the places and the sense of ease with the things I heard others say about him: that he had graduated above them at Groton, that he came from a good New England family. It took me a while to understand the weight of these social associations. But in the years to come I realized how remarkable it was that I got to know Spencer at all. In its literature Harvard prides itself on student diversity, but on campus those of good family find one another rather quickly.

Even as a first-year I knew this obliquely; I knew, for instance, that I would not be invited to join the Hasty Pudding Club or to take weekend trips to the Berkshires. Spencer was my witness to this world, and that was enough. I didn't want to know most of the students who did those things. I saw enough of them in classes and in my dorms. I heard their clubby laughter and saw the careless way they pounded their expensive boots against the floor of the dining hall; it didn't occur to them, I thought, that other students at the college might not be able to laugh at the same things, and it certainly didn't occur to them that other people working at the college might have to work very hard to clean up the snow and mud that had been on their boots. I thought Spencer was different, but then I thought I was different, too.

You shouldn't get so upset, Spencer said, often with a laugh, when I came to him, riled over what I considered to be the thoughtless comment or action of some wealthy student. If Spencer knew the student or his family, he regaled me with amusing stories featuring the student's humiliation. He punctuated the stories with knowing asides and mischievous winks of his bright blue eyes, and then, as I began to chuckle, he would laugh more. It's all a game to them, he said. Just a game. You should try to have fun with it, too.

I must have amused him, too. Was it fun for him, for example, that shopping trip we took together? Or was it as awkward for him as it was for me, standing in the middle of Saks Fifth Avenue in Boston with a growing sense of panic?

In the fall of my first year Spencer escorted me to the Copley Place shopping center and the shops at Prudential Center. I had confessed to him, shyly, that I was clueless about snow. I had seen it in person only a few times on family road trips. I had offered this confession to a few people before, and some good had come of it; a young lady from San Jose, for instance, marched my parents and me to a sporting goods store the summer before I arrived and pointed out the Gore-Tex jacket that I would need. My parents promptly bought it, and I thought that was the end of it. I told Spencer about my fear of snow because I did not know how to behave in it. I did not expect him to look through my closet.

Perhaps he was channeling Aspen and Sun Valley. At any rate, my sweaters were acrylic, my coats were unlined, my boots stood at the height of my ankles, and Spencer shook his head in disgust. We're going shopping next week, he said. This isn't going to do.

That's how I went to the Copley Place shopping center in Boston. The center had branches of all the stores I had, until that time, only read about in *Vogue*: Saks Fifth Avenue, Neiman Marcus, Tiffany and Company—stores I associated with Wealth and Luxury and, especially, Fantasy, since I certainly could not afford their wares and could not imagine a future in which I would have the ability to do so. Unfortunately I did not get a chance to voice my feelings of financial inadequacy, because Spencer strode into every one of these stores without a pause. This Saks looks like a Macy's, he said, storming past the cosmetics department. Look at the design of the departments. No one's organized things properly. We went upstairs to the women's department, and while Spencer sniffed at the coats I acquainted myself with piles of turtlenecks, cardigans, polo necks, shawls, and scarves. I shivered with excitement as I touched the fluffy heaps of cashmere, merino wool, lambswool, angora. Then I spotted a price tag and drew back. I can't afford these, I said with an urgency that startled my companion. I asked if we might go to a cheaper store. Spencer paused, considering how to respond to such a request, and then replied that we could. There were other stores we could look at, he added carefully, but if I wanted to survive a winter in this part of the world, I would have to learn how to invest in—well, in quality fabrics.

What made Spencer different, I thought, was the fact that he had offered to take me shopping for winter clothes. Also, he was involved in community service—still involved, even when there were no college admissions guidelines to worry about—and his involvement was exemplary. Spencer was the leader of a project that provided assistance to working-class Boston families. He coordinated four volunteer teams of students, oversaw the project budget, directed the fund-raising, taught the curriculum, and committed about forty hours a week to these and other responsibilities. Whenever I met him, our first topic of discussion was always the project: the progress of different teams, the team managers, the fund-raisers, the hours he put in, the hours, the hours, the hours, dragging him from his classes and his studying and his social life. I listened to him with great attention. I listened first and foremost because Spencer was talking, and then I listened because I had not joined Spencer's project or any other community-service project during my first year, and I felt confused and conflicted about what I considered a personal failure. I chose to devote myself to the *Harvard Crimson* and other publications, to my classwork, to a boy I was dating at the time. I wanted to learn how to tell stories, to think deeply, and to love. And every time I heard Spencer speak about the work he was doing in a community that needed far more than I even knew how to give, I felt overwhelmed by the poverty of my own desires.

It took some time before I realized that I had never once heard him speak about the families he worked with in Boston. Perhaps that's just because I saw very little of Spencer after a long strange night that spring.

A great deal of drinking was going on that night. There was drinking to begin the night, drinking at the one wretched bar in Cambridge that didn't enforce age restrictions, drinking at a sweaty student party. Some of my friends wanted to stop by another dance; someone I vaguely knew suggested a trip into Boston for real bars, real parties. At the beginning of my first year I would have thought it mad to suggest activities off campus, but by April I thought I had seen enough of Harvard's social scene to bolt back my drink, find my coat, and climb into a cab. The real bars promised in Boston were just as wretched as the ones in Cambridge; the only real party we found was full of current and former Harvard students.

It was an older crowd, so I sat on the sofa and tried to look sophisticated. No one paid any attention to me, except to offer a glass of punch that smelled like paint thinner. It was late. I was tired of drinking, so when I started feeling alone and unsophisticated, I stood up and walked around the house. It was a charming old frame house in a neighborhood that was slowly but certainly creeping toward the tipping point of gentrification. People like my hosts— a young group of recent graduates, two couples, all doing interesting work in the public sector, which they found personally enriching if not monetarily remunerative; that is, it was remunerative enough to afford occasional trips to Saks Fifth Avenue and the rent (or purchase?) of a beautiful home, but not remunerative enough for regular trips to Aspen and Sun Valley and the rent (or purchase?) of a beautiful home on Beacon Hill—lived in this neighborhood alongside the entrenched blue-collar generations. I wondered, as I walked through the large airy rooms, how those neighbors felt about my hosts and their guests tonight. They did not have parties like this, I thought. They did not fill their homes with Harvard graduates who drank and smoked and discussed the night away—in a civilized fashion, to be sure, with no violence, but at an intemperate volume that increased as the night wore on. Their parties were different, I thought, and they shuttered their homes to enforce that difference. As our cab had pulled up I had noticed the unwinking darkness of the homes around us. Perhaps they thought of themselves as the authentic inhabitants of this neighborhood; perhaps they were in fact the descendants of the immigrants who had once lain on cots and mattresses on the floor of the very house I stood in. I tried to imagine the lives of those immigrants as I wandered through the bedrooms on the top floor. Had they crammed into these bedrooms, five and six at a time? Had they filled the space with battered trunks and goose-down comforters and scratchy woolens and small mementos of the old country? Had they fought and cried over the space, the poverty, the crumbled expectations of life in America?

I was standing near a window that looked out on the street. A short, stiff breeze blew in suddenly, ruffling the embroidered curtains. I fingered the curtains and wondered if one of the house's previous inhabitants might have worked in a factory that made ones that looked similar to these. And as I crouched down to look at them more closely I caught sight of a young man on the street. I could not see his face, but I saw that he was drunk—very drunk. He was raving. He was also overturning every garbage can on the street, spilling rubbish everywhere. He did so gently, allowing each can to meet the pavement with a soft clatter, and then he proceeded to kick the garbage bags slowly and carefully, all the while twirling his arms in the air as if he were leading a waltz. I raced downstairs and out the door. By the time I reached him he had started on a pedestrian-crossing sign at the end of the block. He hit the sign over and over again with an open fist. I yelled at him to stop, and he whirled and faced me with cold, furious eyes. Spencer tottered for a moment, still glaring at me, and without a word he turned and slapped the sign with such force that it twisted around the pole.

The next day I spent most of the morning in bed, awake, staring at the grid of the metal bunk bed above me. (In my freshman-year room I had learned something myself about the frustrations of cramped living.) When I did get up, I paced the floor, went back and forth to the dining hall for bits of toast or cracker or apple, and read a few pages of a book without comprehending a thing. In the late afternoon, when the shadows were already starting to deepen, I picked up the student directory. I found Spencer's information and wrote it, very carefully, on a pad of paper. A half-hour passed and I still could not bring myself to call him. I paced and read more. Then, with some hesitation, I picked up my coat and gloves and walked to Winthrop House.

Spencer lived in a room with high ceilings and a view onto the Charles River. He was gazing at that river when I arrived.

His roommate, who had given me a quizzical look when he saw me on the threshold, led me in. Spencer looked up and saw me and offered no resistance when his roommate announced me, and this must have been proof enough. The roommate evaporated. Spencer turned his head back to the river and did not look at me again.

I studied him for a few moments before speaking. Red cobwebs spread across his eyelids and eyeballs. His cheeks bloomed a strange shade of persimmon. He wore only a threadbare T-shirt and a pair of khakis; the veins on his forearms plumped up hazel, and I could see his thick toes, poking white and green into the carpet.

Are you all right? I said.

He shrugged. I guess you've seen me better.

I'm sure you've seen me better, too, I said.

He smiled just a little. It was a long night, he said. Longer than I planned it to be.

We were quiet for a few moments too long.

Spencer, I said suddenly with an urgency that unsettled both of us, were you able to clean up those cans?

Cans? he said.

The garbage cans, I said. From last night. The ones you—the ones you pulled down. Outside the party.

Oh, those, he said. No. No, I wasn't able to.

I knew I had reached the point when it was best to be silent, and for that reason I pressed on. Why not?

Why not? he said. Well, soon after you went into the house, I threw up into the gutter. Then I stumbled indoors and tossed up what was left into a toilet. Vomiting doesn't work for me. I always need to rinse my mouth out several times and, if possible, I try to take a full bath. As it happened, there was a bathtub in the house, and I ran a bath and I lay in it for nearly an hour. Then I put my clothes back on and drank three glasses of water. By the time I finished these exertions it was almost dawn, and I had to get back to campus. I had to finish a report for the project by noon, and it wasn't done. I had to finish it, I had to turn it in. Someone will clean up the garbage, he said, if not today, then tomorrow. It'll be a traffic hazard if it sits there too long.

So, so, wait a minute, I said. The slightest wave of irritation trembled over Spencer's face, and I remembered that Spencer was not accustomed to interruptions. The moment made me smile sadly, and the smile softened my voice and my feeling about what I needed to say:

So you left a huge mess in Boston, in one of the neighborhoods you work in, I said. Then you came back here to write a report about all the community service you've done this year.

It's good, isn't it, Spencer said, and he cracked a smile.

I don't know, I said. I don't know what to say about that.

Spencer's smile faded. He would not look at me, and his face was too puffy for me to detect any emotions. But he squirmed on the futon, and a band of weak spring light settled on his cheek. He looked bee-stung. I know it looks bad, he said. But a deadline's a deadline. I had to fulfill my responsibilities. That was my priority. I'd like to think that we've done enough good to balance out one little mess on the street. We've done a lot over there, those folks will understand. It's not much of a sacrifice, really. And I think we'd all agree that I needed to come back here and finish what I started, write the report, keep the project on line for the next leader in the fall.

And we will have a new leader in the fall. I can't do it, I'll be too busy next year. I'll have my thesis to do, and I'd like to have a social life again, you know. The project's been great, I've learned a lot about management and leadership, it'll look great when I start the recruitment process, but it's time to move on. I'll be putting in enough hours on endless useless projects after graduation.

Oh? I said. I did not know what else to say. Spencer's method of combat was one for which I had no weapons and no recourse.

Uh-huh, he said.

You already know what you're doing after graduation? I said.

Investment banking, he said. It'll take all my time and all my energy and certainly all of my soul. But that's what's got to be done. There are perks to it, you know.

No, I said. I don't know.

He shrugged. For the first time he had no stories with which to regale me, no exaggerated explanations to offer, no humor to share. He would no longer serve as my witness.

Well, he said, there are perks. And I plan to enjoy them.

I see, I said.

He smiled again, and this time the smile lingered on his mouth a little too long, a little too tightly. You always were so serious, he said. Didn't I tell you it was all a game?

Yes, I said.

You're in it, too, he said. So you might as well get what you can out of it.

Yes, you're right, I said, and I knew that he was. Although it must be said that what I got out of it was a long slow walk back to the Yard followed by several hours' worth of weeping on the bottom bunk of the bed in Matthews Hall, and what Spencer got out of it was a $10,000 signing bonus and a starting salary of $85,000 and a position with one of the large investment banks on Wall Street. One of his many tasks was to help the company meet its corporate-responsibility targets. In the years after I heard this I thought about what it meant for Spencer. I wondered if he was searching out at-risk programs in Harlem and Sunset Park; I considered the in-house newsletter he would write about the firm's investments in low-income children's symphonies and ecologically conscious architecture. I thought about him quite a bit, especially since I could not bring myself to talk to him after that day in April. I thought about him when I walked into Saks Fifth Avenue (something that has occurred far too often since he first took me there). I thought about him whenever I went to house parties in slowly gentrifying neighborhoods with sophisticated guests. And I thought about him whenever I heard someone speak of going to Aspen or Sun Valley.

What I thought was that I had expected too much from him, that I had believed in something he was not, something he had never even claimed to be. And as the years passed and I finished mourning those aspects of my friend, I considered that he had been one of the most honest high achievers I had ever known, more honest, even, than me. Spencer could speak his identity narrative with recognition and no shame. It took me a few more years at Harvard to recognize the narrative I had written for myself; as for the shame, it remains under consideration. These were the thoughts that ran through my head when I thought of Spencer during my last couple of years at Harvard, especially as I was sitting in the Afro-American Studies courses there. It was there, in those courses, when all the identity narratives I had heard resurfaced with a luminous intensity.

The Afro-American Studies courses at Harvard were full of bright young black students who were, like me, the products of predominantly white high schools and communities like Almaden Valley. For most of us, college was our first, and possibly last, opportunity to be part of a substantial black community. Throughout our first years and maybe even our second and third years, this opportunity filled us with excitement. We went to the Black Student Union meetings and the tailgate parties and the dances; we took the Afro-American Studies courses; we sat together at special tables in the dining halls. We chose each other as roommates; we went to parties in packs. But after the first year, and even the first term, community membership started to dwindle. Many students simply stopped participating. These defections provoked a great deal of resentment and speculation within the community that remained, and while I cannot speak for the other defectors, I can explain myself.

I backed away because at every function I heard my old grievance again and again and again. The students spoke of being ignored by their teachers and underestimated by their schools. They spoke of being stopped by police vehicles in their own neighborhoods. They spoke of being asked to explain, at any given time and place, the opinion of black Americans on any given topic—rap music, the O. J. Simpson trial, the Nation of Islam. They spoke of Barbie dolls and body image and hair struggles, they spoke and spoke and spoke, and I should note that they did not spin these tales with hesitation or awkwardness. They spoke them freely and fluently, and as they did so I could close my eyes and hear them winning the statewide high school debate tournament, impressing the scholarship panel, holding the audience at the NAACP banquet. Now they sat together and spun these stories, and became angrier and angrier. And I appreciated their anger; I understood their frustration. For obvious reasons I always will.

But after my first year of listening I found my mind wandering as they spoke, wandering into questions that might elicit untold stories about this community. I wondered, for example, why all these students had chosen to remain silent when two young women accused the same young man of sexual assault. I wondered why these students were so silent when young men among them came out as gay, and why they were so disdainful when the campus's gay student group asked for support in a boycott. And I wondered finally what their reactions meant, and how deep they ran, and if those responses might extend to me after graduation, should I choose to write a narrative exposing the suspect practices of their investment banking firm or their community volunteering project. I wondered if their actions were new, or if they had followed them through high school to college, and I wondered how I might have been met at their high schools if I had had the opportunity to write a narrative about my experience there. I wondered, in short, if I should trust the action or the speech. Because I spent so much time wondering about the action, I stopped being able to enjoy what was being said. Instead of listening, I nodded my head and smiled, and I allowed my mind to bring forth my father's voice, and what he said to me during the summer after my graduation from high school:

When I went to Berkeley, he said, I was very aware of what it meant for someone like me to go there. I was very aware of what it meant to go to college then—and there was a different purpose to education then, it hadn't yet become a factory for the mediocre to climb into the comfortable class. College was still concerned with the edification of future American leaders, and I had no point of reference for that. I went because I wanted to learn all that I could and do something for somebody else. I still believed I could change the way things are, and I thought that maybe college could help me do it. My daddy sure thought it could. But still I was a poor kid from Columbus who had made his way to Duarte High School and somehow stumbled through a couple of years at San Jose State, and when I got into Berkeley I carried all those things on my back. And then I went, and it would've been as bad as I imagined had there not been other poor students there, and had we not found comfort in each other and in what we were trying to achieve. So I don't know what to say to you, he said, because I have watched everything change over the years that you have grown. My students are different now. The reasons they come to college are different now. Something has been lost, and I don't recognize what's risen in its place. All I know is that I am increasingly coming to believe that it's useless for anybody to go to college unless you come from a family that's already got money or—lacking that—you share my belief, which I know is rare and old-fashioned these days, about the transcendental power of higher education. I hope that your mother and I have given you and your brother that belief, at least, since it's what we believe in so much and since we didn't have money for you. You two seem to be doing fine, he said with shock. So maybe I've done something right.

At the time of this speech, we were sitting in my father's car. We were on our way to a demonstration in San Francisco: In 1995 the regents of the University of California had outlawed racial affirmative-action policies in the admissions process, with a devastating effect on admissions for black and Latino students in 1997. With some trepidation my father and I were joining Jesse Jackson and some seven thousand others on a march across the Golden Gate Bridge. I do not remember much of what I said to my father or anyone else during the day—I was in a mild state of shock. That speech was the most I had ever heard from my father at once.

And it has stayed with me since, sometimes as a warning, sometimes as history, sometimes as an annihilating judgment of our lives. It helps me on those days when I'm forced to have the confrontation between an achievement and the person I created in order to create it. I share it in the hope that it will help others see that there is a price for the identities we create; there is always a price.

I remember another phone call I received in Cambridge. It was November of my senior year, the time of rainstorms and dark skies and gutters clogged with wilted gold. I was living in a different dorm room, one with thick carpets and a powerful heating system, so I jumped right up to answer the phone. My mother was on the line. She had been at the shopping mall, she said, and she happened to run into an old acquaintance. She wouldn't have recognized her if Amelia hadn't spotted her first. Amelia walked up to her and asked if she was Caille's mom. She said yes, with some abashment, and asked how this woman knew me. Amelia didn't know me—but her youngest daughter, Olivia, was a sophomore at my high school. And though Olivia did not know me, either, she had heard of me at school. My mother and Amelia talked about the school, and in the course of their conversation Amelia asked if it might be possible for her daughter to meet me when I came home for Christmas. Olivia was attempting to launch a black student union, and she was encountering resistance from the faculty and administration. Amelia thought it might be nice for me to talk with her daughter and share some of my strategies for handling the situation.

Of course I had no strategies, but I did have curiosity, and shortly after Christmas I climbed into my mother's Volvo and drove through the streets of San Jose. I met Amelia and her daughter in their small clean home. The house had drafty oak floors and was filled with crystal bowls, shag rugs, and photographs in heavy silver frames. I sat with Olivia on the sofa in the living room. The sofa was white and immaculate and Olivia was jumpy, so I tried to disturb them both as little as possible. This was not difficult as there was nothing new to say. The school still enrolled three black students per class level. The principal still called ethnic clubs separatist. I sighed and looked at Olivia. She was a beautiful girl, slender enough to break in a breeze, and I could tell by her quiet voice and nervous gestures that she was full of the pointless gravity of an ambitious adolescence. My heart went out to her immediately.

I asked her how she felt about the principal's stubbornness, and whether or not any of the other black students would be willing to fight for this club. She shrugged. Most of them had lost hope, she said, although a couple of them were determined to push the school at least a little further. She didn't know about a fight. She wasn't sure what I meant by that word, and she didn't know if that was the best option. She felt that the club could be a good thing and didn't have to be separatist at all. There were white students in the black student unions at other schools, and they seemed to enjoy themselves. It made a good story for their college applications.

I smiled at her, and pursed my lips, and turned the conversation to boyfriends, to college options, to contemporary music, anything to help me avoid the sense of dread that was growing from the knowledge that I would have to tell this story again.

CHAPTER THREE

I HAVE ALWAYS BEEN OBSESSED with stories—the stories with which we abuse ourselves and others; the stories that pour from us in joy or anger or apathy; the stories we invent to provide some sort of exoneration for our lives. I look for the truth of who we are in the narratives we construct around ourselves; I search for clues in eyes and laughs and gestures and pauses. For most of my life there has been no reason behind this. But when I was seventeen years old, I met a man who had locked himself inside his stories, and I decided that it was my duty to help release him. I sensed his pain. I felt his anguish and his mounting confusion; I knew he was struggling, and I thought he was struggling to be good, the way I am. I thought I could help him find the goodness inside himself, because I was seventeen and I thought that it lay within the skills of women to do such things.

Thoughts like these were part of the reason why I slid into depression that year. Thoughts like these were part of the reason why Lila thought I might benefit from meeting Hans in the first place.

She made the introduction during the fall of our senior year in high school. When I look back, I can appreciate her logic. She was concerned about me, and she thought that it would do me some good to meet new people. She thought that the distractions I was using had failed me, and she was correct. One of them was drugs. I had dabbled in marijuana, mushrooms, acid, and alcohol (MDMA, cocaine, and various amphetamines would come later) since I was fifteen, and in my senior year I was becoming a chronic user. This was due not just to increased access (Lila and other friends had introduced me to dealers) but to my other distraction, an eating disorder. One of the few ways I could relax enough to eat was by using drugs.

These two outlets for my frustration had their advantages, but mostly they were just helping me to spiral down further into myself. I thought I needed a silent retreat in order to manage the situation: I was an achiever, and I felt the weight of responsibility with crushing force. Still bound in my identity narrative of righteousness and retribution, I did not feel able to show pain or weakness. So I turned calm, and did what I could to numb myself to the present. Drugs and self-starvation seemed to work, and I daresay that the effects they had on me, in my desperate darker moments, formed my alternative identity narrative during this time of my life.

Lila was sympathetic. She understood something about drugs herself, and the thrill of a quick clean stomach. If we acted as ballast to each other in high school, we also knew how to provide each other a world in which all was permitted. She had grown concerned about me over the last year. She wanted me to pull out of myself and be amused. She wanted me to feel that I had a safe place in which to take drugs and, if I dared, to eat. She also thought that her friend would be intrigued by me and therefore impressed by her; impressing him was important to her, as it would come to be for me.

Hans invited us to a party he was hosting at his house. On that first night we pulled onto the highway with our car windows rolled down, and as the night air washed over me I gazed on the string of homes set deep in the foothills, their lights winking at us like diamonds on a tennis bracelet, and I was filled with a sense of wholeness. I rolled the window down farther, and as we sped along I imagined that those lights were as calm and bright and empty as the stars in the sky, and that I was watching them while I lay on my back in an open field. I might have gone on imagining this forever, lost in some reverie of the night and the light and the wind, had Lila not broken in with information about what lay ahead.

She had first met Hans in 1994, Lila said. She was fourteen years old, and Hans was her then-boyfriend's roommate. I used to talk to Hans in an online chat room in 1994, she said. And he always knew how to make me laugh—not in a crude or awkward way, like his roommate, but in an intelligent and thoughtful way. He struck me as someone who had given a lot of thought to everything—not just politics or current events but human nature and even the state that he was in. And he wasn't always in the state he is now, let me tell you.

What state is he in now? I said.

Well, he's making a six-figure income, that's the state he's in, Lila said. Everything's changed for him. No. Excuse me, I shouldn't have said that. Enough has changed for him, that's more like it. He's positioned himself in the computer industry. He gets up to go to work now, not to do drugs.

Does he know Louis? I said. Louis was one of our drug dealers. Years ago, he had also known Lila's ex-boyfriend, Matt.

Yes, he does, Lila said. But I wouldn't mention it to either of them. Louis doesn't care for Hans.

Oh, I said.

I wouldn't mention it to Camille either, Lila said. She used to know Hans very well. But things . . . things happened between them.

Oh? I said.

She still talks to his cousin, who you'll meet tonight, Lila said. Just not Hans.

Oh, I said.

They can be particular about who comes into their house, Lila said. So I'll have to give you a proper introduction.

At this point the giddy nervousness with which I had been looking forward to the party began to take on an ominous tinge. Camille was a mutual friend of ours; she and Lila were especially close. It seemed unlikely that Camille would know where we were going tonight. Something about that made me uneasy.

Lila must have felt my hesitation, because she added, quickly, I'm not dragging you to some horrible place. At least I don't think so. Hans doesn't get along with a lot of people I know, but he's always treated me with decency and respect. If you feel like something's not right, just let me know. We don't have to stay.

I agreed, but still that unsettled feeling remained with me as Lila turned onto the street and parked her car under a stubby, low-hanging oak. As we walked toward the house I realized that the neighborhood bore a hazy but definite resemblance to my uncle's

Monrovia neighborhood in Southern California: streets lined with aging ranch-style homes, fraying front lawns, sparse streetlights. As a child visiting my grandparents and uncle in Monrovia, I tore through the streets on a bicycle with local children. The homes bore fresher paint then, and the ice-cream man drove by in the summer, and families gathered around portable barbecues on the front lawn. But by the time I came to that neighborhood as a teenager my grandparents were dead and there were no children outside. My uncle had taken to sleeping with a loaded .45 under his pillow. I still own *my* house, he said when I asked him about it, as if that one fact could explain his .45, the illegal bars on all the windows, the broken glass stacked high in the gutters.

Perhaps it could, I now realized, and if I had realized it in the fall of 1996 I might not have been so surprised when I walked into Hans's house for the first time. Nothing in Lila's description of who our hosts were and what they did prepared me for this dank, foul-smelling house; for the stained red carpeting, the salvaged furniture, and the crumbling porch. Young men in black capes and white face makeup milled about. A trio of sullen, pasty girls with crimson nails and black stripes of lip liner were slumped in front of the television in the front room. A card table in the kitchen was lined with plastic cups and bottles of alcohol. A sequence of arrows posted on the walls pointed the way to the bathroom.

No one paid us any mind when we walked in. I took advantage of the opportunity to explore the entire house. There were three bedrooms and a front and back yard, and even then I had enough of an idea of the Silicon Valley real estate market to be impressed that our hosts had the income to rent anything of its size, even if theirs was not the most desirable address. But then I never failed to be impressed by the amount of money our hosts made. I now believe that the reason I was so amazed by the casual displays of wealth I saw at Harvard (the seven-hundred-dollar snow boots, the casual discussion of weekends abroad, the comparison of signing bonuses) is that the first young people I met who had any disposable income to speak of were men like the ones at this party: Billy, for instance, who was fondling a knife with fixed attention in one of the bedrooms I entered (he had already served a prison term for reasons I could never substantiate; he would serve another, for parole violations, as a result of his behavior at one of these parties), and Carl, who was carrying a whip when I stumbled into him in the backyard. They lacked comfort with their money—perhaps they knew that it would not be theirs for long. I mention the men and only the men because all the girls were students and nearly all of us were underage. These men did not associate with women who were their equals in age or income.

But I knew none of this as I walked through their house on that first night. I studied their lighting, as if some answers were contained in the fluorescent tubes in the hallway and the black bulbs in the bedrooms; I pawed through their entertainment as if I expected their stacks of kung-fu and Blaxploitation rental movies to tell me something I needed to know. The other guests regarded my intrusions with blank disinterest, so I kept on, barely noting the enormous computer systems that crowded Hans's bedroom.

As I passed the kitchen I noted Hans himself, brandishing an oversize bottle of Japanese beer as he expounded on some topic for the benefit of the men gathered around him. As soon as I saw him I realized that I, too, had known him before he was making a six-figure income, before he became lord of this three-ring circus. I had met him once, by accident, when I was fifteen years old.

I was overscheduled, of course, but fifteen was the last year of suffering before I could drive myself to the many activities that filled my days. My mother and I arranged a hodgepodge of solutions to my transportation crisis, and one of them was Camille. Camille was a couple of years older than me and had her own car. She agreed to drive me to tutoring lessons or to a family friend's house on occasion. The afternoon I met Hans should have been another calm, uneventful ride. Instead Camille met me in the school parking lot and ordered me to get inside the car immediately. Sensing adventure, I ducked into the backseat without a word. As I did so I bumped up against a man crouched on the floor of the car. He glanced at me and then turned back to concentrate on the back window. As Camille fired up the ignition and tore out of the parking lot he rose slowly from his crouch. He kept his eyes on the window and his body below the line of sight.

In the front, Camille was yelling in fury and writhing in unseen pain. The young man in the backseat with me seemed unconcerned. As my school shrank and faded from view he pulled himself, carefully and deliberately, into a full seated position. Then he turned on me with a cheeky grin.

Hi, I'm Hans, he said.

Leave her out of this, Camille said.

Haven't you told her? Hans said. I think it might be a good idea for her to know what's going on. Just a thought.

We didn't have time, for fuck's sake, Camille said.

Ah, yes, Hans said. I'm sure you didn't. This has all happened in a big hurry, he said to me in a confidential tone. Don't worry, Camille, he said over the front seat. I'll tell her all about it. She looks mighty interested in what's going on. With a smile he glanced at me again. What's your name?

I told him my name.

Nice to meet you, he said. As he continued talking I studied him. He wore black sunglasses, billowy black clothes, and a thick shag of heavily dyed black hair. As he spoke I tried to reconcile the excessive solemnity of his personal presentation with the giggly, gleeful voice in which he spoke.

I've just been robbed, he said. They took thousands of dollars' worth of stereo systems and computer equipment. But they weren't exactly smooth about it, which of course is to be expected, since I'm not dealing with criminal masterminds here. You know what I'm dealing with here? I'm dealing with the kind of criminals who not only tell me that I'm going to be robbed, but they choose to move my things to an apartment where I still have a key.

I didn't know what to say. I suppose I cocked my head and looked at him with skepticism. He glanced at me and flashed that grin. For a long moment he enjoyed his smile, his statement, and the afternoon sun on his shoulders before resuming:

They took it all, he said with a sigh. Idiots. There's no end to the idiots I have to contend with. But I'm not worried. Camille's going to get my things back for me, aren't you?

I can't believe this, Hans, why didn't you do something, Camille was yelling, and I began to grow concerned for her. I had already decided that I was in no immediate danger, and that Hans was too satisfied with himself to venture into a disadvantageous situation, but Camille's distress had not abated. They still hadn't told me what the plan was, and as they shouted back and forth over the car seat I allowed my gaze to drift, very slowly, past Hans to the window. Outside, the streets and stoplights blurred. I didn't recognize the strip malls and fast-food restaurants we were passing. We were driving into a strange part of town.

Hey, Hans said, and I turned my head without a sound. Hmm, he said, thought we'd lost you for a moment. Thought you let your head swim off into the ether. He laughed—a low, cartoonishly demonic laugh—and said, Very good. Good to have you back with us. Along with Camille we've got a quorum.

What are you doing? I said.

Excellent question, Hans said. We're going to go into this apartment and retrieve the things they stole from me. It's my apartment as much as theirs, so it's not like I'm committing a crime. Well, it's not going to be me—they've promised to kill me, and given our previous history I'm inclined to believe them. That's why I've asked my good friend Camille for help.

You're not worried about them killing her? I said.

The question earned an exasperated laugh from Camille, but Hans pressed on as though nothing was funny. Not at all, he said. For two reasons. The first is that if we move quickly we'll be able to clear everything out with no fear of apprehension. There's no one at that apartment right now. I scoped it out over the course of several hours this afternoon. And over the last several months I've plotted their data points and distinguished particular patterns of behavior. There's not a lot of independent moving in this group. They're gone, and if we get there fast enough, there's no chance of running into trouble. According to my calculations Camille's got just over an hour.

Uh-huh, I said, raising an eyebrow.

Not enough for you, huh? Hans said. He released the ridiculous laugh, followed by a short, high-pitched giggle. Tough audience. I like it. Okay, let's move on to reason number two. Camille's not in danger because she's not the one they want. She's done nothing to them. I, on the other hand, represent some sort of threat, some sort of metaphysical challenge. My offense was to abandon their useless way of life. Funny what you get punished for, isn't it?

Camille was driving along the southwestern borders of the city. I recognized the freeway overpasses, the industrial buildings, the cheap Chinese restaurants. On that afternoon Camille was supposed to drop me off at a family friend's house on the other side of town. There I did my homework until my mother, finished at her own job, was able to take me home. The family friend's house was cavernous and quiet, and my family's house was cavernous and quiet, and for some reason, as I bumped along in Camille's car into a dingy neighborhood with noise and theatrics all around me and a hint of menace in the air, I felt a silly smile melt onto my face.

Camille pulled into the parking lot of a twenty-four-hour diner. Hans sprung out of the backseat, stretching and wiggling his body, flexing his toes. You've got the key, right? He said. I gave it to you?

Yes, Hans, now for— Camille began to say. She abandoned the sentence herself without waiting for interruptions. As I opened my car door I saw her shoulders collapse. She bit her bottom lip, then glanced up at me.

I'm assuming you want me to get out, too, I said.

Yes, she said. You don't need to be involved in this. I'll be back as soon as I can.

My right foot was still in the car. I felt Camille's impatience, but I needed more information.

Who are these people he's talking about? I said.

Oh, it's just, Camille said, then sighed. It's just craziness, that's all. These guys are no good, and it's about time Hans got away from all of them. One of the guys involved is Lila's ex-boyfriend. You know Lila, right?

Yes, I said.

Well, her ex is an asshole, and he hangs out with a bunch of assholes, she said. So that's what's going on. She turned the key in the ignition. The car roared to life.

I pulled my right foot out of the backseat and slammed the car door. I would've liked to ask a few more questions while they were both there, but Camille's eyes were trained on the road ahead, and Hans's eyes were trained on the menu posted outside the diner's front door. I waved good-bye to her brake lights, and then I joined Hans.

At the diner, Hans and I enjoyed a quiet hour in each other's company. We talked about the same things we would later always talk about: his family, various forms and methodologies of intoxication, Hans's theories of the human mind, Hans's belief in the power of technology to transform the world, especially after he had implemented his socialist strategies for software distribution. At the time these topics struck me as fresh and fascinating. Hans was charming, sharp, and witty, and the conversational level at the table was so far advanced from what I had grown accustomed to with people my own age that I was too excited to ask him questions that may have been more reasonable for the current circumstances—why had he not involved the police in this theft, for instance. Why he had a key to the apartment in question may have been another excellent inquiry. Perhaps most important, why did he feel that it was all right to endanger a young woman who, by his own words, had done nothing—for his benefit?

In time I would receive answers to all of these questions, even the last one. But it didn't happen during that first party.

Hans paused when he saw me. I wondered if he recognized me from that strange afternoon. But he simply returned to his speech, and I walked into the living room and sat on one of the big black leather couches recently vacated by the three girls. On the coffee table sat a packet of pills, a plastic bag full of marijuana, and a pipe. This gave me pause. I did not know to whom the drugs belonged (nor did I know what the pills were, but that fact was attractive rather than repulsive; had I been able to afford to pay for them, I would have taken them anyway, just to show that I did not care), so I picked up the bag and began plucking buds to fill a bowl.

I was seventeen years old, and I wanted to be a woman very badly. I was unsure of what that meant, but I was trying. I was thin and cynical. Publicly, I scorned authority figures, despite possessing a keen understanding of how to function within their rules and limitations. I smoked clove cigarettes, and read obscure books, and wore dark currant lipstick that didn't suit my complexion. I refused to show surprise, interest, or delight. I fancied I knew something of the world.

While I sat and smoked I thought about Camille. It had been a long time since I had seen her. For some time I had had the suspicion that since she was not obsessed with the concept of womanhood the way I was, she knew something about it that I did not. She was older, but that was just a small part of it. She worked several jobs to pay for her college education, and it was her uncomplaining assumption of adult responsibilities, so rare among people of all ages, that I should have taken as my model. I did notice it as a model, and it worried me that at seventeen I had no adult responsibilities and a nagging fear that I would not behave as well as she did when the time came to assume them.

I noticed her in other ways as well. In high school, for example, both she and Lila had been taking a class with my freshman-year history teacher when my *West* article broke. The teacher took advantage of her captive audience to denounce both me and the article, and before she could finish Camille jumped up and told her that she was wrong. You don't have any right to attack her like this, Camille said. She's just a student, and she's not even here to defend herself. Eyewitnesses told me that Camille's action silenced the teacher on that topic for the remainder of class. No one else, including Lila, said anything in my defense.

So Camille was possessed of a rare quality—which I now recognize as courage—that I appreciated. In fact, I regarded her with awe, though at seventeen I never knew what to say to her. We usually saw each other only when we both had arrangements to see Lila, a circumstance that could only make all of us feel awkward, but I still remember with a shudder something she said to me, in passing, during one of those chance meetings. I had asked her how she felt about working to pay for college, and whether it hadn't made her feel resentful. I think it's important to feel as though you have to work for the opportunities you are given in this world, Camille said. To feel a sense of accountability, like you're not entitled to anything. There's freedom in that, although most people would say otherwise. So I don't have any problem with working hard. As long as I'm not so worn down that I can no longer be surprised by things. As long as I can keep that sense of wonder that children have. You don't have to lose that because you're a grown-up.

These were the thoughts I was engaged in when Hans leaped over the coffee table and came crashing down beside me with a thud. He offered his own introduction: What are you doing in my house?

I struggled for a witty reply. Hans frightened me, but I reminded myself that I could be surprised by nothing. For reassurance, I took a hit off the pipe.

I see you're using someone's drugs without permission as well, he said. Generosity is so undervalued these days, gratitude so rare. But you are young, my dear, and I doubt that you would understand me. So please feel free to help yourself to as much weed as you would like, although I would ask you to be sparing with the pills. They're expensive and difficult to come by.

I did not touch the pills for those very reasons, I said. And I do appreciate your generosity.

It's kind of you to say so, he said. But I may need to appreciate your generosity as well. I'm going to guess that you are the friend Lila said she was going to bring with her tonight. If you are in any way responsible for returning Lila to the fold, then I can forgive you most happily for taking what is not yours, and thank you for your appearance tonight. We've missed Lila, and I'm sure we'll come to find you delightful as well. She told me that you are a thinker; someone who appreciates intellect, logic, and reason. Would you say that this is an accurate description of yourself?

I would, I said, and I would be most curious to discover intellect, logic, and reason in this house.

Ah, he said, I can see that we will get along splendidly. What's your take on technology?

What about it? I said.

You don't strike me as someone who has a great deal of faith in it, Hans said. Maybe you see it as an abstract idea, or a description people use when they talk about advances in the consumer market. Perhaps this last use of the word makes you resentful; you're smart and you know that simply because a new model of a computer or television or food processor has appeared in stores, with trumpets of advertising blasting in the background, the old model doesn't stop functioning. I'd hazard a guess that this has been your primary experience with technology, technology utilized as a coercive phrase to empty your wallet, because you don't look like you've spent years of your life toiling in front of a computer, researching codes, dismantling systems, creating new forms of data. At this point in my life, I can't say that I blame you. Speaking as someone who creates those new forms, I can assure you that it comes at great personal cost—I've had to accept the fact that my life will never be the same as other people's. So in many ways, my dear, yours was the simpler path, the path that I too might have taken, had I the opportunity to do so. But I didn't, and in time I've come to break through my suffering and understand that people like yourself have suffered the true deprivation; a deprivation that will only grow more pronounced as the years go by and the experiments in which people like myself are engaging in, right now, right here in this fine city, come to fruition on a national and global scale. I'm speaking, of course, of computers and information and technology, but what will become of even greater importance is the sea change that will happen in the ways people relate to each other, know each other, see each other. And over the upcoming weeks and months, as you come to be more familiar with the idea of technology with which I'll acquaint you, hold it in your mind that there's something greater going on than the new products and devices that will soon flood the stores; something greater, even, than the money that's flooding this valley.

That was our second introduction. And after such an opening with Hans, when I wandered through the rest of the party I felt that there was little else to see. The others couldn't talk to me like that. They had nothing of use to say at all, or so it seemed to me. The three sullen girls were in the backyard drinking and cackling with Carl, but the fun stopped when I appeared on the threshold of the screen door. I took in their scowls and Carl's whip, and I decided to continue on to the back of the house. I opened a bedroom door and found Billy, alone, crouched down on his haunches as he gripped his knife. He frowned at me when I opened the door. I closed it and moved back into the kitchen.

For a while I stood in the kitchen, where the pack of young men continued their impassioned debate next to the sink. For about ten minutes, I stood on the fringes of the group, increasingly uncomfortable. I didn't know any of them, and none of them seemed willing to interrupt the ongoing conversation—a monologue, really, issued in staccato falsetto by a chubby boy with a black Mohawk and a septum piercing, outlining Kevin Mitnick's revolutionary ethos—so that I might introduce myself. Unfamiliar with the topic under discussion, I could only stare dumbly, and gradually I became aware that Hans was watching me from the living room. When I made eye contact, he grinned and gave me a wink, opening his mouth for exaggeration.

The only moment that alerted me as to what was going on at that house came toward the end. Lila and I were getting ready to make our exit. She told Hans we would be in touch soon, and we walked out with one of the three sullen girls, who was drunkenly weaving toward her car. Outside, the houses looked husked and discarded. The sky was thick blue velvet. The girl asked me if I had had a good time, and I told her that I had.

Yeah, it was a little quieter than the last time I was here, she said, and she seemed disappointed.

What happened the last time? I said.

Oh, Hans was doing nasty things to his brother, she said. Pretty crazy. I think they've got the whole thing on videotape if you want to see it.

That must have been a long time ago, Lila said. Hans doesn't do that kind of thing anymore.

Yeah, said the girl. It was a while back. Then she shrugged. Who knows? He was telling me about another experiment he had planned for the poor guy. Maybe he'll be back. It's hard to give up on your brother, after all. Hmm. Well. Have a good night, she said, and then she waved good-bye to us as she stumbled toward her car on the other side of the street. It was cold; all of our windows were smeared with fog. Before any of us drove away, we let the engines run idle for a few minutes with the windows down so that we might see.

HANS NEVER TOLD ME about his brother. Hans didn't tell me a number of things about himself that I might have found useful, but in a way that didn't matter because I knew, as soon as I left that first party, that I would be coming back. And I did go back, almost every Friday night. At the time I told myself that I would go back for the safe haven, for the opportunity to indulge my impulses. I told myself that it was refreshing to spend time with people who were actively thinking about the world and what we could do about it, even if I disagreed with their conclusions. These were thin and unconvincing reasons, even then, even to myself. I went back because I had felt something in Hans, and I thought he had felt something within me. *Listen,* he would tell me. You're the only one with some sense around here. And I may not always be able to speak with you about these things.

And speaking was what we did. There was a strong sexual spark between us, but our physical relationship was mild—in part because

I saw on several separate occasions the tiresomely dramatic conclusions that played out at Hans's parties when circumstances between him and other girls soured and I wanted no part of it; in part because I recognized that not only was he not the right person, but this was neither the right time nor the right place for me to gain sexual experience; and in part because Hans had other plans for me. *Listen,* he would tell me. You're the only one with some sense around here. There are things you need to know.

Were there things I needed to know? When I look back, all I can think of are the things he failed to tell me. He failed to tell me about the person he had been when he first met Lila. In 1994 Hans was an overweight, unemployed high school dropout. Intimidated by traditional social settings, he retreated to the world of his computer, where he created a mythical persona for himself in online chat rooms. It was through one of these that he met Lila, then fourteen years old, and Matt, the alcoholic skinhead who was to become Lila's first serious boyfriend and Hans's best friend. Matt adopted the dress, manner, and doctrine of skinhead groups without ever joining an official organization. This hesitation was due not to any doubts about the beliefs he would be required to espouse (he tried to intimidate people constantly, Lila said; he shouted threats and racist abuse even when he was sitting on the sidewalk with a Styrofoam cup, shaking from the d.t.'s, desperate to buy a beer) but because he found the group tenets of cleanliness and order too exacting. Matt's first love was controlled substances, not the Glorious White Race, and while he could encourage Hans to explore both of those subjects freely he could not assist Hans in securing the necessities of life. That task fell to Lance.

Lance was Hans's unassuming older brother. The first of the family to attend college, Lance earned an associate's degree and began working as a computer programmer in the early 1990s. Despite his quiet personality, Lance leveraged his technological expertise and his exposure to the burgeoning online world to fashion an alternate personality for himself—a personality that was aggressive, knowledgeable, capable. This new personality gave Lance an increasing sense of confidence that must have underlined his younger brother's feelings of depression.

Sometimes I wonder what their home must have been like during the year Hans spent sleeping on his brother's couch. It would have been a silent home, certainly, for both men spent hours at their computers, and I cannot imagine Hans articulating to Lance anything like his explanation for why he followed in his footsteps: Suddenly, he said, my brother had friends all over the country and in different parts of the world. They discussed projects that seemed of the utmost importance, all the more enticing because they were beyond my comprehension. This was a marked change from the way things used to be; Lance had always said that my brilliance was blinding, and that beside me his intelligence was no brighter than a lone, flickering Christmas light. It is true that I had always been the clever one, the one with all the wit and all the ideas. But now I spent my days at Matt's apartment frying on acid and my nights sleeping on my brother's couch, while he made more money than anyone in our family had ever dreamed of earning. He spoke of travel, and of property, and I began to look at him as having some authority in these matters. And as I watched from the couch I felt a sense of mounting outrage.

One night Hans ingested nearly thirty tabs of acid. It should have killed him. Instead it affected his brain in such a way that he believed he had discovered a unifying theory of universal organization, and the answer was technology. He quit using acid immediately. He abandoned Matt just as quickly. He focused on learning all that he could about computers, and Lance encouraged him. Lance bought how-to books on coding for Hans; he provided him with secondhand computers; and slowly Hans educated himself. He found an immediate source of inspiration in the open-source movement, epitomized by the free computer operating system Linux.

Traditional open-source development occurs when a group of programmers and software developers pool their skills for the purpose of creating a free, functional computer operation—often one that is meant to serve as an alternative to consumer products, as Linux was meant to serve as an alternative to Microsoft Windows. Throughout the 1990s, a widely held philosophy about open-source development prevailed, one that claimed open-source development occurred outside the economic market. Because many software developers, programmers, and hackers lived in conditions of economic stability, so the philosophy went, they chose to reject the corporate, late-capitalist practice of consumer software production in favor of a revolutionary "gift" ethos of widespread software sharing. This philosophy gave many programmers the sense that they were the members of a new cultural vanguard. It dovetailed nicely with the fact that the work those same programmers were doing for the corporate sector was in fact the new economic vanguard, and they were compensated accordingly, but the questions that this juxtaposition raised were not questions that many, Hans included, stopped to consider.

As soon as Hans developed his skills sufficiently, he started contributing to as many open-source projects as he could find. After about nine months, his programming work caught the eye of a recruiter for one of Silicon Valley's oldest and most prestigious computer companies. A few months later Hans had a job with an annual salary of $75,000. He rented his own apartment and bought a car. He lost weight and stopped seeing Matt, although he took with him his friend's penchant for antisocial behavior, as well as his own dearly nursed memories of marginalization and misery. Proclaiming himself a lifelong student of technology and human behavior, he performed experiments whenever he developed a hypothesis. He enjoyed experimenting on different subjects; Camille said she had been one the year after she risked life and limb to collect his stolen belongings.

For several months, Camille said, he led me on in what I believed was an honest romantic relationship. He took me out on dates, drove me to appointments, asked me about my dreams, slept with me. He told me that I was beautiful, that I was special, that he had never been so fortunate in all of his life. I'm sure that you can imagine the rest of what he said, because I can no longer bear to do so. It does me no good to remember such things, because they always lead me back to the night I went to his house to watch a movie and he pulled out his notebook and informed me that it had all been an experiment to prove his hypothesis about the immense properties of the female ego. For his evidence, he recited the things I'd confided in him, the reactions I'd had during intimate moments, the behavior I'd exhibited when being treated to flowers or surprise visits or a kind ear. After he told me that, I turned away and walked out without a word. I vowed that I would never speak to him again.

In solidarity, Lila did not speak to him for more than a year. Then he called Lila and told her that he had changed, and she agreed to come to a party at his house. I suppose during the time that both Camille and Lila were out of contact with him, Hans turned back to his favorite subject of all: his brother, Lance.

IT TOOK ME MANY YEARS to piece all of this together. Hans told me only those parts of his history that made him proud. The rest of his backstory I learned from strangers' casual remarks at parties, bitter mumbles from mutual acquaintances, and long conversations with Lila. And still I would accuse Hans of many things but not necessarily of lacking familial loyalty, because my own experience with him showed me something different. During the year that I was his friend, Hans had a faithful companion—his cousin Carl. Their family's heritage was French and Vietnamese; with his slight build and Asiatic features, Carl favored the Vietnamese side. By contrast, Hans was tall, pale, and broad, with a face that looked as though it had been shaped by thumbs. As Lance had once done for him, so Hans did for Carl, providing him with a bedroom in the south San Jose house and employment through his contacts. Carl was supposedly a contract programmer and software developer, though I never heard any testimonies about his talent. It didn't seem to matter.

Carl's main role, as I understood it, was to provide Hans with a foil for his various ideas, plans, projects, and experiments.

Then there was Hans's relationship with his parents. I never had occasion to meet his mother, about whom Hans would say only that she was legally insane. But I did meet his father once. He had the meek contemptuous patience of someone who has spent too many hours engaged in a particular form of waiting: waiting in lines for government services, for emergency-room healthcare, for the nine o'clock opening of the check-cashing store. My most vivid memory of that meeting took place about halfway through it, when Hans mentioned a desire to spend some time in Britain. His father jumped to his feet in a state of agitation. Scurrying around the room, he repeated over and over again his opinion that this was a dreadful idea. When Hans pressed his father for an explanation, he stopped moving and stared at his son. Isn't it obvious? he said. They don't speak English there.

According to Hans, his father had dropped out of school in order to work in the orchards and orange groves that were the San Jose metropolitan area through the late 1960s. He picked and planted, eventually gaining management authority over other workers, but when the orchards started to disappear, he was unsure of what to do next. Unqualified for the industries that replaced agriculture industries like defense and computers and real estate development; industries that required specialized skills or higher education—he worked wherever he could, usually in the low-wage service jobs that were available to a man at the middle of his life and the end of his health. Hans said that he was extraordinarily abusive toward both of his children, and eventually Hans stopped speaking to him. His father, Hans said, belonged to a class of people who were no longer useful in Silicon Valley. He spent most of his time watching bad television shows, walking to the drugstore to get prescription refills for a growing list of ailments, and—because such habits die hard—screening his calls for bill collectors. He was not yet sixty years old.

Hans told me this story over and over again. It took me some time to realize that he did not share any stories of childhood, family events, or what his father had been like as a role model. It took me even more time to realize that this was the only story that Hans had about his father and that Hans was writing the script of not just his father's past but his own future.

THIS NOTE OF FATALISM stood in stark contrast to Hans's techno-optimism, and to the facts then at hand: the fact that Hans was earning a six-figure salary, and the fact that we were passing through a California boom. California booms are brief, cyclical, and extravagant; they contain exaggerated possibilities, which is in keeping with the state's image of itself as a miracle place where the best of everything is just around the bend. Every boom here strikes the residents with an incurable sense of amnesia, not simply because this is a state and a county where the soil is toxic to the seeds of history but also because California booms have a habit of altering the landscape in excessive ways. The gold rush created the urban centers of Northern California. Another boom at the beginning of the twentieth century, in agriculture, turned the state into a greenhouse; when that greenhouse needed to be destroyed in order to make way for subsequent bonanzas in real estate, aerospace, and Cold War defense, residents complied with all due speed. The hand-wringing over this destruction wasn't to come until a generation later.

Now, at the end of the twentieth century, came technology, a boom that seemed even greater than the ones that had come before because of its unlimited global audience. But the historical fact is that California had been primed for the technology boom since the state's inception. It had been primed by its relentlessly speculative attitude toward the future, by its obsession with progress and improvement, by its long-standing interest in science and mechanics, but most of all it had been primed by favoritism from the federal government. The federal government had allowed gold rush–era miners to loot its land without paying a single dollar of tax into the national Treasury in the 1840s and 1850s; the federal government had provided California with exorbitant sums for water and agriculture projects throughout the twentieth century; and it was the federal government that supplied all those jobs in aerospace and defense that led to the growth of California's middle class in the 1950s and 1960s. So the fact that it was the federal government that provided the seed for the Internet, through the Department of Defense's ARPANET project in the 1960s and 1970s, might not have come as a surprise to those in California who have a fondness for history, but there were very few of those people in the Bay Area during the mid-1990s. History had no place in their script. A history of our economic interdependence with others only brings with it the fear of obligation to others. And history could not account for the Important Things going on in the garages and labs and venture-capital boardrooms of Silicon Valley. If anything, history was a useless weight—slowing down the forces of Progress with its negative energy; demanding attention for all sorts of people, including those who are part of the class that is no longer useful.

Theirs was a script I never believed, though I understood why many others wanted to, had to. It promised a world of opportunities, even for men who lacked traditional education, like Hans and Carl. If a high school dropout like Jim Clark (he later went on to earn not just a bachelor's but a master's and Ph.D., but that was never part of the story) could launch three multibillion-dollar companies— Silicon Graphics, Netscape, and Healtheon—in two decades, then perhaps they could live without ever screening their calls from bill collectors. If a man like Bill Gates could quit Harvard to chase after his dream, then perhaps they were right to live by their wits, to see education as something for those who lacked faith in their own abilities to turn cables and chips and code into something miraculous. If a man like Jerry Yang could team up with his college roommate and create a billion-dollar company—Yahoo!—in a campus trailer, then perhaps they were correct to maintain a prospecting attitude toward the idea of making a living, to jump from company to company in the hopes of striking it rich. To believe this script, they had to find a way to ignore the auxiliary costs it came with: the surreal prices for real estate and rentals in the Bay Area, the spiraling cost of living and the decreasing quality of life, the fact that economic mobility goes in two directions.

Every once in a while, I brought up these auxiliary costs to Hans, but doing so only brought rebuke down upon me. He told me that I was allowing myself to be distracted by details—the sign, he said, of an immature mind. To a girl who was as eager to be grown-up as I was, such an accusation represented the gravest of insults, and left me far too engrossed in my own wounded pride to point out the obvious flaws in the matrix of rationalizations he had formulated to explain why this California boom would be different from all the others.

Things are going to change because of technology, he said. I know that this is hard for you to understand; you have not seen any of these changes yet, and you are too smart to believe what the media tells you. But try to envision it with me—try to imagine what a society will look like when everyone is empowered by free access to technology and information, the very things our economy is predicated on making them pay for. We are a cultural vanguard, and it has all come about because of the revolutionary actions of a few dedicated hackers who stopped what they were doing long enough to realize that they were living in an economy where scarcity was a thing of the past. Since they had what they needed to live—and they were happy with that—they didn't need some yuppie job with some massive company. They decided that they would offer up their services for free. Stay with me here, because this is the most difficult piece of the puzzle to understand. It was the hardest step for me to understand, because it is truly the most revolutionary of all actions to take, is it not, to decide that you are going to give away the skills and products for which you could earn enormous amounts of money; to decide to offer people an alternative way of life. While I was working on these projects with others from all over the world, it was understood that none of us would earn any sort of copyright for the programs we were producing. It was understood that we would dedicate hours to these programs and not demand any rights of ownership, even to the least penny, in exchange for all of our work. And in fact we received nothing, nothing but the enhancement of our own egos, which I will admit is an extraordinary bonus. It is extraordinary to be part of a movement that is searching for ways to break down all the haughty claims of intellectual property and opportunity cost and trademark, all the insidious things companies employ to keep people trapped in petty, narrow relationships to themselves and the world. It is extraordinary to build a gift economy on the ruins of an industrial one. It is an extraordinary thing to tell people that they are now in control of the information that has been out of their reach for centuries, as a result of geography or poverty or access, and that it has all come about merely because a few people decided to think differently about the way they were relating to other people. I suppose there is no amount of money that can match that feeling.

He supposed there was not, but I supposed there was, and in his case I supposed it was $75,000, his starting salary at the first company to hire him. When he got that first job, he lost the opportunity to spend hours and hours on open-source projects, and he entered a world where intellectual property and copyright and ownership were the gravest of interests and revolutions were not. I tried to point these things out in a way that would not cause him to take offense, but reality can be offensive. So I usually settled for a simple, emphatic negation of what he said.

I don't believe this is going to change anything in the way people relate to one another, I said. I don't think that technology is going to improve anything for us.

I could never explain further, partly because by the point in the evening when Hans had pulled me into his room for an impassioned monologue I was usually too incapacitated by alcohol and pills and weed and food to think and articulate clearly, but mostly because the answer was right there in the details Hans was so eager to dismiss. These were not just the details of life in Silicon Valley but the details in Hans's living room, where Carl was groping his fourteen-year-old girlfriend before a willing audience, and the details in Hans's notebook of experiments. To point these things out would have indicted not just Hans but myself. It also would have shut down Hans's willingness to communicate with me, and I believed I was making progress at encouraging him to open himself to life, to real learning, to joy. I was afraid that if I pointed these things out to Hans, he would just attack me. He would accuse me of bad faith and passing judgment, and the specter of that fight frightened me. What frightened me even more was that it would have meant the end of our dialogue, and I had convinced myself that I was important to Hans. I thought I was different from the other girls he knew. I had convinced myself that because he did not call me names and he deigned to share his ideas with me (He respects you, Lila said once, as much as he can respect anyone), I had some special kind of power over him. And I believed that a woman should have power over men. To point out the obvious reason why I did not believe free access to technology and information would change anything might have led to the end of my power.

PERHAPS MY ARGUMENT might have gone further with Louis, my drug dealer, and not just because he despised Hans. My feelings for Hans were complicated, but my feelings for Louis were simple. I liked Louis. It was a simple thing to like Louis; he had no interest in harming anyone. That was what had made him a target for Matt, Lila's ex-boyfriend, and Hans. Louis had once frequented Matt's apartment when he was a fifteen-year-old high school dropout, feeling lost and unmoored. He had been kind even then, Lila said, and while I was dating Matt I kept thinking that I should be dating Louis. But I was young, and what interested me about men was their capacity for cruelty, not kindness. Louis was ejected from Matt's house after a year and much abuse. Lila looked him up after she broke up with Matt. I met him during my sophomore year in high school.

In theory, Louis sold a variety of softer controlled substances with an emphasis on the natural and the hallucinogenic. In practice, his methodology for obtaining these drugs was notoriously unreliable. Lila and I learned quickly that we could not depend on him for any drug aside from marijuana, but he dealt that with a passion that made his failings in other areas seem unimportant. He sought out exotic strains and custom blends, and, like an organic farmer, he supplied his customers with the best of whatever was in season. As a bonus, he had little regard for rigorous measurements. I recall very clearly my disappointment when times changed and I had to purchase weed from new dealers: Louis's "eighth" was the common interpretation of a "quarter."

Perhaps he was generous because he smoked so much of the product himself. I can remember only one occasion when I saw him sober, and that was the morning after a small gathering I attended in his bare apartment in Sunnyvale during my junior year of high school. It was a few days before my seventeenth birthday, and he, his friend Dave, Lila, and I smoked upwards of twenty bowls' worth of Northern Lights Number Five before passing out on the linoleum floor.

Being in a state of constant intoxication was costly, Louis said, but then so was the alternative. In fact, inebriation had saved him from physical danger more than once. He told me his favorite story on this theme: One afternoon his suppliers drove down from Humboldt to confront him about what they believed was a betrayal. My suppliers, he said, are this good hippie couple who got into marijuana farming for the love and affection they felt toward the drug, not for the money they could make. They spun me a beautiful tale about growing up crushed by small-town expectations, and in their early twenties coming to California, or the California they found in the Haight-Ashbury at least, and believing they were in paradise. And they told me about the drugs they had tried, and how they had come to the conclusion that marijuana was the best, because it opened you up to peace and love without leaving you immobilized. Of course, I was touched by all this, and whenever I saw them or thought of them, it was always with a smile in my heart, and so you can imagine my hurt feelings when they stormed my apartment and demanded to know why I was stealing from them. They flew in with threats and fury; and the woman was cawing like a pigeon, and I was so stoned that it took me a couple of minutes to understand that this was a dangerous situation. They thought I was cutting them out of a lucrative deal because I had been buying so much product, and somewhere in the fuzzy recesses of my consciousness I realized I had to speak up, because many, many men in such a position have been killed for smaller errors in communication. Fortunately at this moment the man, who was towering over me with the back of his hand raised for a blow, paused to look at the redness of my eyes. He asked me to speak, and I did, with great difficulty. I tried to explain the movement of their product, but I may as well have been reciting the rosary. He shouted to his wife that I was too stoned to know what was happening, and she walked over, and both of them stood stroking their graying ponytails in disgust. Then they left, and when I called a week later, it was as if nothing had happened. So I truly believe that marijuana can lead to peace and love, he said with a laugh.

Perhaps he was generous because he smoked, or because he believed in peace and love, or perhaps it was because he did not depend on marijuana sales for his income. Louis had left school at the age of fourteen in order to devote himself to his computer; when I met him five years later, he was earning more than $100,000 a year at one of the valley's best-known start-up businesses. I can't say what it was about technology that captured Louis's interest. Like

Hans, he was familiar with the world of open-source development; unlike Hans, he had no unified theory about how technology would lead to widespread societal change. When I think back on it now, he had very few theories of any kind. This may be the most profound and refreshing way to live, and perhaps that is why I retain affection for him, unchanged by time or distance.

Whatever his passion for technology, it was an intensely private one, as private as the way he chose to spend his money. Like many young men who made fortunes during this era, Louis was unconcerned with the outward trappings of wealth. He shopped at thrift stores for furniture and ate greasy pizza and Chinese takeout. He dyed his hair blue to match his eyes, and wore it in long, matted plaits that he twisted himself. He wore heavy old boots and big black clothes that fanned around his small frame. He drove an ancient, mud-spattered truck, propped on off-road wheels. He rented a series of small, austere apartments all over the Bay Area. He didn't travel or buy gadgets. He spent most of his time at work.

I wondered how Louis managed every day to go to his job, where he earned larger and larger bonuses but faced more and more marginalization. The company for which he worked prided itself on obliterating hierarchies—in all the media accounts I read, the company founders boasted of working alongside their employees in the same hive of cubicles—but Louis's employers gave him an office at the back of the building. His employers requested that he work there, and suggested that the back entrance would be the most convenient way for him to get to his office. To compound the insult, they encouraged him to work night hours. When they asked me that, Louis said, I got the distinct impression that my face sure wasn't the face of the company, or at least not the face they wanted to show to any client who might be walking in the front door. He complied with their requests. Perhaps he expected little from the people who made decisions at these companies. Once, in the most casual manner I could muster and with a keen interest not to discourage his efforts, I asked Louis why he sold marijuana. He did not offer a reason but simply said that his interest in drugs was as long-standing as his interest in computers. Both things, he said, help me understand the world in different ways, and one of the greatest frustrations I have is that only the computers are considered acceptable. Of course, I try to remind myself that it's just a question of who considers what to be acceptable. For if the arbiters of acceptability in my life are people like my colleagues, swooping in from the East Coast with their khakis and their tennis rackets; people who were in college changing their majors from economics to computer science so that they could cash in on what was happening as quickly as possible while I was at home creating my first software designs, then I really don't care.

It was a bold statement, fired by passion, and it was one for which Louis paid full price when he was called to back it with action. And from what I had seen of Louis's home life—which I must admit is very little—he had some experience with the misery that came from trying to fulfill someone else's standards of acceptability. He came from a broken home, which is the typical California story, but what was more memorable was the way he spoke of the attempts made by his mother, a European immigrant, to provide for her family in a country and culture she did not fully understand or necessarily believe in. He offered few details, but I sensed her feelings of helplessness the moment I met her. Our meeting took place on a radiant afternoon during the spring of my junior year in high school. I had met Louis only once or twice before, and I was excited about going to his apartment to complete a transaction. Lila and I washed our faces and combed our hair in the bathroom after school, and then we drove to Milpitas. At this time he lived in an apartment block there, one of those sprawling multi-story stucco complexes that seem to multiply every time you blink your eyes, and some days just driving inside the gate was enough to provoke in me a sense of panic. That panic swelled when Louis's mother opened the door. Whatever my anxiety was, hers must have been worse, for at the sight of us—two slim, scrubbed girls in pleated plaid uniforms, the picture of young earnest prosperity—she recoiled into the hushed dark of Louis's apartment. Lila and I stammered our greetings, but she recoiled further. She did not meet our eyes. We stood there as she backed away down the unlit hallway, silent except for the shuffle of her house slippers.

HER IMAGE CAME TO ME every time I crossed the threshold of Hans's door with her son's merchandise in my pocket. I wanted to ask Hans if he had ever met her; I wondered if perhaps they had traded stories about their families. I never asked. There were a lot of questions I wanted to ask but didn't. There was the question of Hans's biting contempt for his co-workers: Do they all buy those khakis at the same store, he said, and are khakis on the rack next to smugness, and did they all decide to pick that up, too? I noticed that his contempt increased on the days Hans learned of other people's promotions. Then there was the question of the girls he and Carl took pleasure in seducing. The girls were all spoiled and suburban, in many cases the beneficiaries of a father's newfound wealth in the computer industry. I wanted to ask how Hans believed technology could find a way to inspire a revolutionary ethos among these people, but I didn't. I didn't push very far on this problem, choosing instead to blame it on the drugs and the alcohol and the ever-present undercurrent of violence at Hans's house on Friday nights. It seemed like a dangerous place to ask genuine questions, and it was. But now that I think about it, it was not the danger that kept me quiet. It was that I already knew the answers. Hans, who could not hear anyone's questions, who could not hear anything, perhaps, except for the alarm ringing louder and louder in his head, was answering the questions with everything he said.

Once, for example, I asked Hans about what I believed would be the logical outcome of a society in which everyone had free access to technology and information. If you stick with the assumption, which is huge, that most people would have personal initiative once they gain access to these things, I said, then there would be no need for a class of people to develop and maintain technology. Everybody would just do the work himself. After a long period of community education at the beginning, no one would need engineers, programmers, or technicians. There would be no need for start-ups or technical universities or venture capital. There wouldn't even be a need for hackers. Maybe I'm being cynical, but I can't imagine that anyone would seek to bring about a world in which their skills would be obsolete.

I'm glad you brought that up, Hans said, because I've given it a lot of thought. I think it goes along nicely with the semantic issue I have noticed in the media. People call this a boom, or a gold rush, as if people like myself were simply the first wave to discover a mother lode. Both of these points miss the idea that there's something crucial going on here that will change everything. Personally, I don't see less of a need for us; I see more. We'll be needed to create new ideas and new technologies. We'll also have to continue pushing the boundaries of the old ones. And I'm not so naïve as to assume that everyone will want responsibility for their own technology. Some people will lack the time, others the interest. Those people will also need us to simplify their lives. There is no danger of obsolescence if the change is permanent and far-reaching, as it'll be.

And if it's not? I said.

And if it's not, he said. He took a sip of beer and he smiled at me. We were sitting on the couch in the waning hours of a party, and he turned his head to look at what was before him. He cast his smile on the television set, fuzzy with the poor print of an old movie. He cast his smile on the kitchen, littered with plastic cups and wadded napkins and spilled alcohol, and on the guests who were splayed in various postures on the kitchen table and on the floor. He cast his smile on his cousin, who was sitting on the opposite couch. Carl had given his girlfriend the night off in favor of another girl he met a few days before; they slurped each other with sullen indifference. The girl had brought along a glassy-eyed friend who was eighteen years old. Her friend wore purple eyeliner and short, henna-dyed hair spikes. She had been trying to attract Hans's attention all night. He cast his smile on her now. She smiled back, and he gave her a big, obvious wink. If it's not, he said, then at least I've enjoyed myself.

OUR DISCUSSIONS were not always so calm: I was stubbornly attached to my skepticism. I see too many people with your attitude, he once said. And people with that dumb resistance to change and progress will prevent the full effects of technology from taking place. You claim that resistance is necessary for morality, or private property, or privacy, or the sacredness of this or that; any of these arguments will work for you, and they're all the same.

Most nights he would leave the debate there, as an effective enough dismissal of the forces against which he was struggling, and we would join the others in the living room. Hans and Carl would laugh too loudly and compete over who could issue the better insult about a person they loathed. I would sit next to Lila and nibble on cheeseless vegetarian pizza. To block out the dreadful sensation of an expanding stomach, I fretted over the question of how I presumably came to hate technology. The evening would end quietly, with all of us too engrossed in our internal distress to act out any spectacular misbehavior, and I would begin my weekend with a sense of apprehension that I found impossible to shake. That sense remained unrelieved until the night Hans, beset by some hidden conflict and full of the most perfect calm I had ever seen in him, challenged me to admit that white people were the dominant race and technology was yet another example of their superiority.

It's no accident that white people are where they are today, Hans said, for the logic it makes, given their early mastery of technology, is whole and complete. It took the superior intelligence of white people to recognize the potential of the ship, the written word, and the gun; it took white people to recognize the power of all these things put together. I'm sure you have heard the revisionist theories of people with an interest in promoting other races; I'm sure you tout those theories yourself. You know, theories that point to the Chinese as being the inventors of guns, for example, or claims that great scholars of the Roman Empire studied in Africa, that sort of nonsense. Unlike a number of people who believe in white superiority, I see no need to lash out against people who propagate superstitions of that kind. They can keep their fantasies, because the truth is obvious. It doesn't matter if the Chinese emperor was hosting target practice in the imperial palace for centuries before white people laid their hands on guns. Because when they did, only white people had the reason and the imagination to recognize what a gun could do. And a technology is only as good as its user. Considering that white people built the greatest empires this world has ever seen, and they built them from locations with no natural resources, their intelligence is clearly superior, their dominance justly deserved. And the technological breakthroughs that white people are producing in Silicon Valley right now are just one more illustration of that fact.

We were sitting on his bed as he said this. Lila, Carl, and the others were entertaining themselves in the rooms outside. As he finished his statement Hans got up from the bed and stood in front of me. His eyes darted over my face; his hands curled into fists. He stood above me and watched, watched, watched for my response full of anger.

And I struggled to do it, because the anger was certainly there. What was even more present, however, was my feelings of betrayal and humiliation; and perhaps they won out in the end, because I was gradually coming to the realization that no amount of contention for the opposite side of an argument that I believed was not merely untrue and illogical but ultimately repulsive and cowardly would serve to make my feelings disappear. I did espouse theories of the sort Hans had ridiculed. More to the point, I espoused moral ideas, forms of speculative doubt as to whether or not terms like *progress* and *superiority* had anything to do with the material examples with which they are associated. In my head, these moral ideas were stronger than any facts I might struggle to recall at that moment of stunned submission. And moral ideas are not logical. They are not logical, they are not witty, they are not reasonable. So I said nothing.

Later that night, I wobbled out of Hans's house and climbed into my car for a long, lurching drive home. I wasn't fit to drive that night; I wasn't fit to drive many nights and more than a few days over the course of that school year. But I did anyway, because my situation was not such that I had blacked out or could not see what was in front of me in its real dimensions. Those things had happened, too, quite often that year, and the memories settled heavily on me as I picked my way through the living room. Carl was passed out on the couch with one hand plastered on the breast of his girlfriend. He said she was fourteen years old and a resident of Los Gatos, one of the wealthiest towns in America. She had waist-length hair and diamond earrings and a cold-eyed lascivious stare. He bragged about her many times before bringing her to the house; he was pleased with himself for finding one so young. When he did bring her she seemed all that he said she would be. I always imagined her living in a house in the Los Gatos hills or the unincorporated Santa Cruz mountains that loomed over the town. It would be a spacious and airy house, surrounded by streetlights and oak trees in the hills or redwoods in the mountains. She radiated a sense of neurotic entitlement which suggested this sort of upbringing, but that was not what frightened me about her. It was frightening that she once brought an escort to Hans's house: her seventeen-year-old sister, who alternated between telling me about the fifteen pairs of boots she owned and attempting to convince her sister that there were better things for her than Carl and a foul living room in south San Jose. It was *really* frightening that she chose to keep pawing Carl in full view while her sister pleaded with her. She was defying her own best interests, and in that I recognized myself. She had merely chosen a different path to the womanhood we both so fervently desired.

Those were the thoughts in my head as I walked out that night, and there was another thought, too: I asked myself what I had to gain by coming back. I knew that the reason I kept doing so was Hans, and the power I believed I had over him. I told myself that because I was different from the other girls he knew, and certainly the other people of color he knew (I do not believe he knew any others besides his own family, but that was not the point), that I could use that power for good. I told myself that I could help him understand how he was being misled by the techno-utopian rhetoric that he had constructed around himself like a tin-roofed shanty. I believed he really wanted that kind of self-awareness. I told myself that I could imagine possibilities for a better way of life independent of technology. I even told myself that next time I could articulate a clear counterargument to his polemic on white superiority. For if he chose to follow that polemic to its logical conclusion, it would inevitably lead to what the skinheads call the Day of the Rope, and I believe that if that day is coming, they might come for me first but they would come for Hans later, and his family, and even the friends who had introduced him to that particular idea of Progress. I believe something else now, too: that the real reason I kept going back had nothing to do with all this. It was just about power.

I just liked feeling that I had power.

SO FOR THE NEXT TWO MONTHS I continued to go to Hans's house on Friday nights and buy drugs from Louis. Hans and I didn't speak about his racist diatribe, but our conversations changed. I had less to say to him. He, in turn, spoke to me less about ideas and more about the mundane. He tried to make me laugh with jokes and silly skits he acted out with Carl. We didn't look each other in the eye. I grew certain that he was losing patience with me.

This frightened me, and not just because I feared the attacks he would unleash if I stuck around too long. All I could think was that I had somehow failed to break through to him.

I was still puzzling over the proper response to Hans when circumstances changed. I had already been seeing less of Louis for reasons of convenience. He had moved again. He had a new job again. His new home was in Redwood City, thirty-five miles north of San Jose, and his new employers encouraged him to work regular hours. It became an enormous challenge to coordinate our transactions. So with great fondness, I wished him well. He seemed excited about his prospects at a new company, which he described as clever and open to change.

The next year Louis was driving south from a routine purchase trip to Humboldt when a highway patrol officer pulled him over for a broken taillight. The presiding judge at his trial promptly sentenced him to seven years in prison, in accordance with the mandatory-minimum sentencing laws of the state of California.

I stopped seeing Hans that spring as well, a couple of days after Camille attempted to file charges against him and his cousin for gang rape. Lila told me the story a few days after it happened. Camille said that Carl had invited her to their home one evening with the specific promise that Hans would be absent. She was surprised to find both of them there when she arrived. She was eager to leave, but they urged her to stay for a few drinks and a few stories. She agreed to talking—not drinking—and she spent an hour with them while they drank beer and shared jokes and stories. Then Hans disappeared into his bedroom and re-emerged with the video camera, his notebook, and some duct tape.

The police said she had to get a taped confession, Lila said, or she wouldn't have a case. It was too late for physical evidence by the time she got to the police station, and without evidence the case amounted to her word against theirs. If the case even made it to court, the police said, the defense lawyers would savage every element of her sexual, mental, physical, and emotional history in order to gain the upper hand for their clients—that was the common procedure, they said. If she wanted to pursue a case, she should get a confession. So she agreed to call Hans and Carl from the station. The police had been bragging about their new recorder. I remember reading a brief in the newspaper about equipment upgrades at the police station; this recorder was supposed to be the latest technology. Two clerks were operating it when she stepped into the booth to make the call. As soon as she got on the phone Hans and Carl confessed everything. They recounted everything that they had done. Carl even said that he had expected her to lie back and enjoy it. It was all that was needed to condemn them in any civilized court of law. But when she stepped out of the booth the clerks were panicking. They had made a mistake; they were still learning how to use the machine. They hadn't recorded the call. They asked her to try again. How she found the strength to dial the number again I really don't know, but I do know that they would confess nothing the second time.

Camille told Lila this story over a weekend, and on Monday morning Lila searched all over school for me. She tracked me down after first period, and we missed twenty minutes of our next class while we walked through the halls and Lila told me what had happened. When she finished, I was shuddering, so we walked to the outdoor courtyard. I drank in the cool spring air in gulps. For a few moments we were quiet, and then I looked at her and she looked at me. There are many, many aspects of this story that disturb me to this day, but perhaps the worst one is this: I was not surprised.

LOUIS SERVED FOUR YEARS in federal prison. Upon his release, he swore off all drugs and alcohol. He decided to go back to school and learn whatever he had to in order to get back into the technology industry. When I saw him in 2004, he was attending community college and working in a mechanic's garage. He was clean-shaven, polite, and well-spoken; he had many theories about many things. As always, it was a pleasure to see him, although he did not remember me. He told me not to view his lack of recognition as an insult. There are many things I don't remember from that time, he said. I can't even remember what I've chosen to forget.

Lila and I stopped speaking to Hans, of course. Lila even confronted him; they had a nasty yelling match outside his house. And though Lila told him that I didn't care if he lived or died, he sent me an e-mail message in 2002. I don't know what provoked this—maybe he felt that enough time had passed and we could all forget—but in this message he shared the news of his life with me. He had shared the fate of many computer programmers in Silicon Valley after the technology boom came to an abrupt end in 2001: He was laid off. He had begun to hear that many companies were moving what programming work was left overseas, especially to India and

China. He was in the process of weighing his options. In the meantime, he was unemployed, living with his girlfriend in an apartment
in San Jose, planning to start a company of his own.

I sent him a reply with a question about Carl. He said that their
association had ended. I've moved on from all that, he wrote, and I
believed him. Then he asked if we could meet for dinner, to share
some of the better memories we had. I wanted to believe that we had
better memories to share. But it was 2002, and the technology boom
was over, and when it came to hearing stories I too had moved on
from the ones I once liked to hear.

CHAPTER FOUR

HANS WAS THE BEGINNING.

His dream was to achieve financial success and psychic stability through technology. I understood that he was deluding himself, but I did not see that I was dreaming, too. I had believed that I could become a woman by saving him from himself. I had been depending on the intrinsic goodness of others to make its appearance at the times when it was most needed. I had been depending on my strength, my pragmatism, and my sense of justice. And I had been depending on California to save me, as it had saved my parents. Hans was the beginning of the end of those dreams. A remarkable group of young people I met around the same time I met him finished the job.

Many of the false conceits I held about myself and my home were swept away at some point during my tenure as a youth writer at Pacific News Service, a news and commentary wire service specializing in the concerns of the Pacific Rim. In 1991, executive editor Sandy Close established a division called Youth Outlook, which she envisioned as an opportunity for marginalized young people to report news and write commentary for mainstream media outlets. Through a wire service, Youth Outlook reporters see their work printed in newspapers around the country, including the *San Francisco Examiner*, the *Washington Post*, the *Chicago Tribune*, and the *Akron Beacon-Journal*. Their articles are collected into a monthly newspaper, which is distributed free of charge to local high schools. Since its inception, Youth Outlook has expanded to include programs for writers in Bay Area youth detention centers, a local radio show, and a local television program. Sandy has executed all this on a shoestring budget with a staff of teenagers who are homeless, hustling, imprisoned, addicted, in and out of school, in and out of foster care, in and out of mental institutions. (She also takes her work home: Many Youth Outlook writers who would otherwise be living on the street have found a room at her house, often for months at a time.) Occasionally a teenager who lacks hardship credentials shows up at Youth Outlook with a desire to write, and if she intrigues Sandy a little, Sandy might agree to take her on. That was how I managed to join.

I knew nothing about all this when I showed up for my first meeting, in the fall of 1995. I was simply a sixteen-year-old seething with feelings of despair and restlessness and found that writing was another way, even better than drugs, to mute them. I went to Youth Outlook because I had heard it was an outlet for writing; my introduction had come through a young man named Stanley Joseph, who gave a speech to a group of educators. Stanley was a Haitian immigrant who joked incessantly and worked at least three jobs. He was good-looking, he was polite, he was articulate and upwardly mobile, and in certain situations he was the perfect public face for an organization like Youth Outlook. This speech was one of those situations and Sandy knew it. When my mother came home and told me about Youth Outlook, neither she nor I imagined that the other writers would be any different from us in either social class or aspiration.

I could not have been more surprised when I walked into the office for the first time. Now, of course, my reaction makes me laugh, and it makes me grateful. Youth Outlook was my introduction to a life outside of abstractions. I had been living in a world that was conceptual: There was a chip on my shoulder about the obscure slights and humiliations I had endured, about the vague and inchoate assumptions and expectations people hold about me because of what I am and what I am not, because of what I have and what I do not have. When I walked into Youth Outlook for the first time I had not yet ruminated on the idea that a conceptual life, particularly a life full of resentment about concepts, was a luxury provided to me by the hard work, sacrifice, and good fortune of my parents. I had not yet become friendly with the notion that my ability to develop, recognize, and quantify—and therefore harbor resentment about—all the concepts of which I was aware was the function of another luxury, my education. I did not know that while people of my economic class have the luxury of creating and fighting about concepts; it is the hardship of people like the staff of Youth Outlook to live them. I had never imagined myself as privileged, in part because privilege trumps righteous indignation. Fortunately the staff at Youth Outlook shook me free from most of my moorings, starting with that one. For at least the two-hour duration of our staff meetings, I had to cease being angry about my plight in the world. It was the first chance I had ever had to imagine the peace that comes when you let go of resentment for good.

It began as soon as I walked in the door and came face-to-face with Ladie Terry. Ladie was the receptionist at Pacific News Service; it was her role to act as gatekeeper, taskmaster, and first line of defense. As her eyes flickered over me and her mouth puckered I grew unsure as to whether I would be allowed to make the breach. What're you here for? she asked. Her voice was low and serious. I stammered a response, and her eyes flickered over me again. In the back, she said finally. Behind the cabinets. I turned to go, and felt her eyes on me with every step.

Later on I learned more about Ladie. She grew up poor in precarious circumstances all over the Bay Area. Rather than dwelling on the deprivations she endured, she fought to feel beautiful—not the easiest task, she argued, for a woman who was poor, dark-skinned, short-haired, and voluptuous. Hence her name, which she had adopted as a teenager; hence her gut-wrenching articles about her attempts to maintain self-respect around men who made her feel as though she were disposable; hence her eventual conversion to Islam, where she took comfort in the beauty that modesty can bring. When she began coming to the office in her draperies—first alone, then with her husband and children—she seemed overwhelmed with relief. I thought of her relief for a long time after I learned of her death in 2002. She had been riding in a car that was in a collision. Some of the passengers lived; Ladie was one of the ones who didn't. For the first time things make sense, she said the last time I saw her. Things are falling together. They're starting to matter.

I picked my way through file cabinets and potted plants and over-flowing cubicles. I was so nervous, and the office was so cramped, that with each jeté and plié I executed I grew more and more certain that the next spot where I dared to place my toe would be the one that sprang the trap. I pictured the office snapping shut around me. Ladie Terry would be at the head of my captors, I thought grimly, taunting me with cheese.

I turned the final corner that would lead me to the meeting (rows of folding chairs and the hooded backs of young men floated into my line of vision) and stumbled into a group of men, three of them, leaning against a file cabinet. They had been mumbling among themselves, but they stopped immediately and stared at me. Their expressions were a mixture of disbelief and curiosity, which could have been in response to any number of concerns, but I was still focused on the trap and the cheese. We exchanged one glance, and I quickly reversed course.

One of those young men smirked a little while I was backpedaling. He went by the name of J.G. A few months later I asked him why he had laughed at me that first day. His response, which I remember with particular clarity because it was the same afternoon he tried to remove my panties (I was sitting down on a patch of grass when his hand slid up my skirt; no one had done that to me before; I froze in terror, shook my head vigorously, and did not dare to speak), was some nonsense about the dazzling impact of my beauty. Though I wanted to, I did not snort in derision. And it was well that I did not. My suitor (temporary; my father quickly disabused him of such notions) got into trouble the way most of us get into our shoes. I had heard rumors of theft, drug possession, statutory rape. When I asked him, he shrugged off all the charges with a dreamy expression on his face. He had spent some years living in San Francisco's Tenderloin neighborhood, he said. Homeless sometimes. Sometimes not. The neighborhood was full of prostitutes and junkies and runaway kids who spent their days huffing glue and drinking cough medicine, and it was difficult and dangerous for everyone. While he lived there it had been hard for him to think about long-term consequences. Sometimes it was still hard, he said. He paused as he was telling me this (I was offering him one of my best sober nods) to take out a plastic bag of marijuana. We were sitting in a bright, crowded park. It was a weekday afternoon. Mothers were pushing strollers around us; children were jumping off the swing sets. He smiled at me and blinked into the sun and painstakingly rolled a joint. Then again, he said, and he sounded very pleased and dreamy as he said it, maybe I just don't care.

(J.G. didn't remain with Youth Outlook for very long. Eventually he exhausted Sandy's patience and left her home, where he had been staying. Once he left, I never saw him again.)

When I got to the back of the room, I stood wordless for an immeasurable amount of time in front of those gathered there, letting them inspect me while I tried to keep my knees from shaking. Nell Bernstein, who was leading the meeting, must have noticed my knees, or she must have guessed—Nell's powers of perception border on the clairvoyant—because she asked someone to fetch me a chair. When it came, I positioned it next to the mildest-looking face I could find, and I sat with my hands in my lap.

Welcome, Nell said. I'm nominally in charge here, but you look like you'll be able to find your way without me.

She was wrong on both counts. Nell was modest about her guidance and overconfident in my self-possession: I could not have found my way at Youth Outlook, or through the nasty aftermath of the first article I wrote for them, without her. Even now, when I am suffering through a moment or a day or a month when I am so crushed by the realities of life that I cannot imagine tying my own shoes, I try to draw on Nell's remarkable reserves of calmness and competence. She steered our wobbly crew with the greatest of ease, and it was not until she was gone, and there was new leadership, that I realized how difficult it must have been.

I dared to smile at the friendly face next to me. A broad, wicked grin spread across it in return; Lyn Duff knew just how to smile, and just how to act, to keep those around her off-balance. Most of the time all she had to do was be herself. When I met her, she was a heavyset young woman with close-cropped hair and an unfussy, androgynous wardrobe. Like me, Lyn had a materially comfortable childhood in a suburban locale; all that ended for her when she came out as a lesbian in her mid-teens. Her family's response to this news was to enroll her in a camp that prided itself on fixing the sexual preferences of confused teenagers. Lyn was insubordinate at the camp and defiant to all suggestions that she was passing through a temporary phase. When she remained unconverted, her parents asked her to leave their home. She was sixteen years old when she complied. When I met her, she had been living with friends and out on the streets for more than a year.

She was remarkably calm and lucid about it all. My parents say that I've been brainwashed by a radical lesbian agenda, Lyn said. I've tried to tell them that I am in fact that agenda, but they are convinced that I am lost, and so I'm fending for myself until they find me as I am. In the meantime, I've got to be that agenda in a society that's still homophobic, and take responsibility for my worldly needs. The upside of my situation is that I've learned how useless we become during a life in the suburbs. All my instincts had atrophied. And I'm not the only one. In the suburbs we all depend on the same uncreative action to fulfill our demands: shopping. I can better understand the longing for convenience the longer I stay away, but I'm growing more and more repulsed by the desire for a clean, unsullied life.

(Lyn has since told us that she has changed her perspective on some of these issues. Several years ago she converted to Christianity and attended, of her own free will, a church-sponsored program designed to cure homosexuality. She had a successful course. She is thin now, and she wears dresses and she has long hair and she dates men. She has many suitors. I expect that she will marry soon.)

These were my colleagues. I wish every budding writer could have my good fortune. We were never short of stories at Youth Outlook; we could always mine the depths of our own experience. There was some mutual apprehension at first. (I didn't speak to anyone besides Nell for the first two meetings. As for the general consensus on me, I heard it echoed time and again in the words of my friend Kevin Weston: I didn't know what to think, man, he has said to me. Except that you looked awfully civilized. Like you cared about where people went to school and shit. And this was a place for people who hadn't been to school. And shit.) But within a few months I was driving up to the Youth Outlook office as often as I could. Sometimes I had a story to work on, and I told my parents that I needed to use the organization's resources in order to do my job. Sometimes there was a meeting, and I told my parents that I needed to be present in order to voice my opinions and stay informed about what was going on.

These were excuses. Youth Outlook was an economical operation designed for people with no fixed addresses. The writers showed up when they could, and the only available resources were rotary-dial telephones and outdated word processors. My stories excited me, and I worked hard on them, but they had nothing to do with the reasons I went to the office. I went to see who was there and what was going on.

That something was going on was inevitable. There would be a fight between writers, or a party for someone newly sprung from prison, or a new venture to launch, or a new couple making their shy debut after we had seen them groping each other in a corner during a youth conference in the civic center. (We were speakers at these conferences and, I suppose, role models of a sort. I worry for the next generation.) I came to the office and sat quietly in a corner to watch the day's dramatics unfold, fascinated by everything. Sometimes it ended there, and sometimes the excitement moved out of the office. If I could, I went with it, and it is through those experiences that I began to see the Bay Area for myself.

I began to understand why my parents believed in California.

I saw the beautiful tumult of a culture that allowed a group of young people like us to move from an ad-hoc hip-hop battle in Golden Gate Park on a clear, breezeless afternoon to a black-tie dinner in a Union Square hotel that night. The splendor of a geography that allowed us to move from the tropics to the mountains to the desert when we went to different prisons to give writing workshops. The tremendous sense of hope and possibility that still remains—despite all evidence to the contrary—and that allowed a woman to imagine an organization that would pay the least accepted elements of society to tell their stories with honesty and humor, and maybe, as a side result, inspire them with a new profession.

I found the embodiment of all these ideas in a Youth Outlook writer named George. It was some time before I met him; when I joined Youth Outlook in 1995, George was busy with other pursuits. I was probably out selling crack, he has since said to me. That was a pretty good season, which surprised me. I thought for sure it was over on the street and I was going to have to switch my inventory. But it kept on and on.

When we finally did meet, it was at a nonprofit organization's gala in a downtown reception hall. Sandy had reserved a table and encouraged us to bring our parents. My mother and I, dressed in our understated finery, were seated next to Ladie Terry and her aunt. Our other tablemates were Ri'Chard Magee, who stood six foot four without his crown of dreadlocks, and his stunning mother, who had supermodel proportions and cheekbones that could shred a block of ice. Needless to say, my mother and I were paralyzed. And then George walked in, calm and parentless, dressed in casual clothes because they were all he had. He greeted everyone at the table and sat down. As the program wore on, I stole glances at him. He was polite and quiet, even aloof, but when they announced the first

course, I noticed that he was studying the place setting with a terrified expression. I caught his eye for a moment and smiled. Slowly
and carefully, he smiled back. From that moment we have never
stopped interpreting the world for each other.

It has been a strange friendship, to be sure. At first George maintained his aloof exterior and assumed the role of my informant and
protector at Youth Outlook. (That boy got himself into all kinds of
shit, he said after J.G. disappeared. He shouldn't have been hanging
around you anyway. And don't think I didn't hear about him trying
to touch you.) Even after I relocated to Cambridge, he would occasionally call to check in. I would trudge back to my dormitory after
fourteen-hour days of classes and meetings, my head swimming
with Habermas and student gossip. As I unwound my scarf and
turned on my computer I would absentmindedly rewind the answering machine. When George's voice would crackle over the
speaker, I'd drop my scarf and bolt to attention. Hey, Miss Millner,
he would say, just calling because I thought you might like to know
a couple of things going on out here in the Bay. (In Cambridge, I'd
close my eyes and feel the vertigo of topping a hill on Divisadero
Street and tipping the nose of my car over the edge while George sat
in the passenger seat smoking a blunt and mumbling about a cryptic
summons that had come over his pager.) Cash and them left for At-
lanta. Not sure if you would care, but if he owed you money it might
be time to start thinking about your options. Oh, and I don't know
if you heard, but Santa got sent back to Soledad. On a sell. So now
he's got two sells and I don't think we'll be seeing him anytime
soon. Stupid, man. That nigga knows better. But there it is. So let

me know if you want to send him something, me and some folks are getting a package together. Another crackle from the phone wire, and the message was over as abruptly as it had begun. My knees would soften, and I'd grab the back of my desk chair.

I made a point of visiting George whenever I was in town for holiday breaks, and after a few years of this he began to crack jokes, pontificate on his solutions to the world's problems, and generally act more comfortable. We still fell into our old roles—especially when, out of nostalgia, we sat on the curb in the alley behind the old Pacific News Service office and shared a blunt. (I was so convinced for so long that you didn't do any ghetto shit, he said. I'm so glad you do. As long as you don't get tangled up in any real ghetto shit, you know what I mean? No heroin, either. You'd like that. You'd really like that.) But by this point we were able to smile at those roles, too. Still, George's primary role in my life remained that of a lifeline between me and the Youth Outlook community we had known. I did not learn anything about him until after that community was destroyed.

Early one morning in November 2004, I answered a telephone call from George. I was living in San Francisco, but I was single, whereas George had three children and a complicated relationship. We did not see each other very often.

I picked up the telephone, and George's voice came pouring out of the other end. He said that he needed a ride to San Francisco's General Hospital, and he knew that I had a car. If I would be willing to take him, he said, paused, and said again that if I would be willing to take him—

I agreed to pick him up at once. General Hospital is in Potrero Hill, a sunny neighborhood in a far corner of southwest San Francisco. The Victorians are old, and they keel over on steep hills that wind together in a maze of one-way and dead-end streets. Originally the neighborhood housed middle-class families and longshoremen; as the city's ports declined and the navy base closed, Potrero Hill became known for gang warfare and a few notorious public-housing projects. George lost one of his cousins in a shooting there in the early 1990s. Most of the neighborhood has now been gentrified almost past the point of recognition, but in terms of its geography it remains a neighborhood that has been crushed and tossed out to the bay like a tin can. We were lost as soon as we turned down the first dead-end street. Rather than getting frustrated, we took it as an opportunity to inquire into each other's lives. George insisted on hearing about my life first. Sitting in the car with him again made me feel so comfortable that I rambled on and on about the small petty problems that had become outsized dramas in my existence (I was heartbroken as usual; I was frustrated at my job; I didn't believe I had enough money for the upcoming Christmas holidays). At some point I paused to ask George about his father, whom he would be visiting at the hospital. We had been friends for nearly a decade, and I had never heard him speak of his father at all.

He paused and took a long moment to speak. When he did, it was in a burst of eloquence, as if he had a speech rehearsed, although I doubt it was a speech for which he had planned an audience: My father is drying out after an extended cocaine binge in Portland, Oregon, he said. I didn't think that even he could find trouble in

Portland. I remember that city being real temperate in every instance. I saw it when I was a teenager, during the time in my life when my grandparents thought they could clear my mind of all it had already taken on by showing me parts of the country that were green and peaceful. And I remember Portland being lush with rain and sleepy with comfort, and I was amazed that people could live that way, and it made me wonder if someday I might be able to raise my kids in such a place, so they believed that's the normal way to live. But things worked out the way they did, and my father was the one who lived in Portland. He was the one who got to wander in the mist and the clean streets. Or at least he did until the woman he was living with let him know that he couldn't stay in that city anymore. So he came back here, to San Francisco General, and I'm glad you're here with me, because the last time I came to this hospital over an issue with my father, I didn't think I was going to make it out of here with all my faculties, you know what I mean? I was four years old and I had shot myself through the hand. It's one of my first memories. I meant to shoot my father, who was pistol-whipping my mother on the other side of the room, but I didn't know how to aim yet. The bullet ricocheted off a telephone a few feet away and tore through my left palm. For a moment I stood in the kitchen by myself, amazed at how a circle of the linoleum floor opened up through my hand, and then the blood came. I didn't scream, and they kept on, taking their fight outside. Meantime I gathered a pool of blood around me. It was dark outside, and the pool in the kitchen was dark, and I remember thinking that maybe the dark outside would overcome the dark inside and just swallow me up. I was still in the middle of these questions when my mother ran in the house and saw what I had done. She screamed, and to this day I believe it was her scream, not the bullet, that brought on a sudden pain, which dropped me to my knees in the dark pool that was spreading all over the kitchen floor. She grabbed my wrist and dragged me up the stairs into the apartment where my father had taken a break from beating her in order to do a few lines and play a quick poker game with his friends. My father was leaning over the folding table when we ran in, and I remember thinking that this must be a momentous occasion indeed, you know what I mean, because he jumped up so fast that he smeared cocaine across his face. And even at four years old I knew that my father didn't make quick movements around his cocaine. We sped to the hospital, and we were driving so fast that a policeman pulled us over. I can't imagine what they thought when they saw the beaten woman and the four-year-old with a bullet hole in his hand and the man with cocaine smeared across his face, but they were kind enough to offer us an emergency escort to the hospital before they took my father aside for questioning. So my last memory of being with my father at the hospital we're coming up to right now ends with me screaming on a gurney in the emergency room while I watched the police being a bit rough with my father just outside the sliding doors. It's strange, George said—his voice sharp with the emphatic tenor of a sudden thought—when my father called me yesterday to ask if I could meet him here, I hesitated. Not because I'd have to see him, but because I'd have to see him at this hospital. Something about the combination of him and me and this hospital gives me pause. I almost lost my hand that night. I'm afraid I might lose something more the second time.

We were sitting in the parking lot of the hospital. A light drizzle began to fall; the nurses and assistants stubbed out their cigarettes, hooded their heads, and walked under the eaves. In silence, George and I watched an emergency-van driver cover the patient he was unloading with his own jacket before he wheeled the gurney through the sliding doors.

You don't have to go in, I said. I can drive you somewhere else.

George was quiet for another moment. The sound of rain on the car roof had swelled into a dead, hollow tap; George had no coat. But he opened the car door and turned to look at me. Listen to me, he said. Talking like I'm still scared of something that happened when I was four years old. It was just a bullet a long time ago. It wasn't the last one for either of us, and we're both still here. Now he's at this hospital, and he wants to see me. So I'm going. He swung his legs out of the car and stood up. Then he scrambled back into the car and kissed my cheek. I want you to stop worrying about those boys, I heard, and then he was running through the rain.

I watched him pound through the sliding doors, and then I sat and continued to watch. After a few minutes of sitting alone in my car, listening to the rain pluck my heartstrings and my nerves, I turned the key in the ignition. As I drove away it occurred to me that the only valid complaint I should have expressed to George was that I was the only one of the people we had known at Youth Outlook who had the means and the availability to drive him to the hospital. Nearly everyone else had disappeared. Even George himself—who would not have needed a ride to the hospital had he still been able to afford to live with his family in the low-income Hunters Point neighborhood in which he grew up—was gone. In 2001 he had found himself suddenly and irrevocably forced to leave the city if he wanted a home. As for the others, some of them had died by accident or design. Some had disappeared into space with the stubborn obscurity of the transient; some had been asked to leave Youth Outlook. But most of them had disappeared because they had been squeezed out of San Francisco. Our community had broken down over the price of real estate.

Gentrification was one of the Bay Area's defining stories during the 1990s. The nine-county region saw a thirty percent increase in housing prices from the middle of 1998 through the end of 2000; in the area known as Silicon Valley (including Santa Clara, San Mateo, and portions of Santa Cruz and Alameda counties), the average price of a single-family home rose 87 percent, to $617,000. The San Francisco rent board surprised no one when it released the figures it had found for that city in the year 2000: Housing evictions had doubled over the previous four years, rent had jumped fivefold over the previous two years, and residential vacancies stood at less than one percent. The de facto situation on the streets was even more stark: Entire neighborhoods, even cities, were transformed in just a few years. Many of the displaced left the Bay Area for good.

By the time I found the community at Youth Outlook it had already started to break down.

So I may be more sensitive than the average person when questions arise about the links between shifting neighborhoods, affordable housing, wealth discrepancies, and displaced communities. I'm also more likely to place myself in residence in a shifting neighborhood. When I lived in Brooklyn, for example, there was no need for me to live on Twenty-first Street between Sixth and Seventh Avenues. I could have rented a room in Boerum Hill, or Williamsburg, or even in the Park Slope area west of Prospect Park, which had been through a comprehensive gentrification process and made no gestures toward affordability. But I chose to live in a neighborhood that the upwardly mobile called southern Park Slope and the entrenched residents continued to call Sunset Park. (Since 2004, real estate agents have been calling it Greenwood Heights.) Every night while I lived there I walked the streets with a pen and a notebook. After my first few strolls I began recording the procession of new businesses into my community. As my list moved quickly from corner groceries and automobile-repair garages to health-food stores and bistros, I felt the first rise of panic; when I started to see Pilates studios, I abandoned my walks altogether and started spending the evenings in front of my computer instead. I typed up a list entitled "Suggestions for Decoration," annotated it with descriptions of each building, and distributed copies to local graffiti artists. (Among the first people I met in my neighborhood were these shy young men. Most of them were underage; they usually lived with their parents in increasingly desperate circumstances. They knew better than anyone what was happening around us; they felt the consequences, they told me, not just in the policing of their work but in the policing of their friends and neighbors. Still, no one took up my challenge. All of them chuckled and returned the list.

I suppose they had their own plans for Brooklyn, which could not be accomplished from a jail cell.)

All that I can say about my response to the development of Greenwood Heights is that at the time it made sense to me. It made sense to me because I had sat in my car with George near the public housing in Potrero Hill. On a clear, brisk morning in 2000 we watched the sun rise over the corner of Twenty-fifth and Wisconsin, bleaching the buildings and lighting the windows like signal flares. I asked him if he was still living down the road in Hunters Point. As we sat in my car, unsure of whether to gaze on the startling picture of Potrero Hill's warehouses and barracks warming to the sun or on the fantastic vision of the bay spread out at our feet, George told me no. We were staying over there at my cousin's house, he said. Me and my kids and their mother.

He fell quiet, and I shifted in my seat to look at him. He stared at the bay. I watched the curve of his mouth stiffen as he felt my stare. After a moment, he rubbed his eyes and opened his mouth and out it poured, unbidden. You know how it is here, he said. You know what things cost, what I had to do to get them. And I was trying to clean all of that up, so that my kids didn't have to know me that way. I was trying to hold down some job, anything I could get, and make it happen that way. My cousin wanted to support me, so he let us live with him in Hunters Point. We were living with my cousin and my uncle who got AIDS, all of us in the house, that was part of the problem. I'm not mad at my cousin for getting fed up with having all those people in his house, especially my kids, who I am proud to say are the finest noisemakers outside of a Cracker Jack box. But if that was it, he should've said it, and we'd have left pleasantly and in fine fashion. But he didn't. He had to go on filling my head with shit. And then my uncle who got AIDS—check this out, right, my uncle who got AIDS moved in after we had lived there for four or five months. He told my cousin that he should sleep in the spare bedroom and my cousin should put the five of us where he was sleeping, on the couch in the living room. Now, if you can decipher an equation for how five people fit on a living room couch more efficiently than one, then you, my friend, deserve a place of honor in the Mensa hall of fame. Right next to the nuclear astrophysics section. My uncle who got AIDS said things like that to my cousin all the time—that we should sleep on the couch, that we never cleaned up the house, that my kids were disturbing him, *whoomp whoomp whoomp*. And I ignored him because I knew he was on some bullshit, and from my perspective he was blaming me for his own failures. Man, he kept me from sleeping with his fits and his tantrums and his needs and his wants and his this and his that. What he needed to do was investigate why he couldn't die with dignity. Man, I'm telling you, if a person can't live with dignity, they can't die with it either. But anyway—I knew he was trying to wear down my cousin, but I figured that my cousin could see what was going on. My cousin had always told me that his priorities rested in making sure our family stayed intact in this city. San Francisco's the closest thing my people got to an ancestral home, feel me? And he knew that. He told me that family was his main concern; he told me that his home was mine; he told me all other kinds of bullshit, which I don't care to remember and which I sure don't care to repeat because I'm getting mad all over again. So I thought we were cool, I thought he would disregard nonsense, and I guess I didn't pay attention to the way my uncle who got AIDS was wearing him down. It all became clear the night my uncle grabbed my son by the throat, though. Boy, did it ever become clear. It's amazing I didn't kill that man. As it was I let him know that if he ever thought about putting his hands on my son again, I'd kill him a long time before AIDS would. He flew off, crazy-like, started screaming about how I had no right to live at all; I remember him screaming about that. The rest is all *whoomp whoomp whoomp*, because he slapped me in the face. And that's when things made a swift reversal, you know what I'm saying? A swift and complete reversal. I don't even remember what happened. That's how mad I was. My girl told me that she ran downstairs because she heard me yelling. The kids came after her, and they all said that they saw me pounding his head into the sofa. At first my girl said she was hollering at me to stop, and trying to get the kids to calm down, but then my cousin ran into the room with a cutting board and knocked me over the head. I crumbled onto the sofa on top of my uncle, and when I rolled to my feet, my girl was trying to wrestle my cousin to the ground. My kids swam right in after her. I know they're going to need some neuro-linguistic reprogramming after all this, but when I think about it, I bust up laughing. My little soldiers. Taking on the bad guy for their daddy. So yeah, there we were, flopping and shoving and yelling and tugging. I got to my feet, pulled the kids away. And as I was helping my girl to stand my cousin came at us with the cutting board. I told him to stop. Stop, man, I said. The fight's over. Fight's over. And my kids were panting behind me, and I was still holding my girl back, and my uncle who got AIDS was running his yap, but my cousin ignored all of them and looked right at me. Get out now, he said. And that's all you get. I'm not going to be responsible for you anymore. And I started to say, what? Like we were still having a conversation. Like my opinion mattered at that point. Like my situation mattered. Like any of the pretty words he had said to me about us being one family, one need, mattered. Shit. You know what he said to me? He said I wasn't worthy of the family name. Like we're some dynasty. Man, I went upstairs and I packed our things into plastic bags from the grocery store and I marched my unworthy behind right on out of there, with my kids crying and my girl threatening right behind me. All five of us just holding our grocery bags and tumbling out into the night. And all I could think about was how I was going to have to raise my kids outside of this city, which I love with every bit of marrow and bone in my body. This was the city I wanted them to know. It's all my family's ever known. But I think that was it for us.

George and his family went to east Oakland. Oakland lies across the bay from San Francisco. While it possesses stunning views and some inordinately wealthy residents in the hills, as a city it grew around the Navy and the docks, and it has never quite been able to shake off its reputation as San Francisco's working-class step-brother. After the docks declined, Oakland went through a long period of uncertainty and trouble. When George moved there, the mayor of Oakland was doing all that he could to encourage down-town rehabilitation and business investment. He offered corporate subsidies and an expanded police force, which sought to contain disorder and violence to east Oakland, a part of the city that is still shaking off the crack-induced blight of the 1990s. So George and his family went to east Oakland, and I went back to Harvard. And because I heard this story from George around the same time as something called the Living Wage Campaign was unfolding on the Harvard campus, I believe that my feelings toward that issue may have been heightened.

By that point I had made my decisions about what Harvard was about and who it trained its students to be. As I had pontificated drunkenly during many late nights, it functioned best as a finishing school for people with the highest personal ambitions. What I learned at Harvard was how to behave as though I had gone to Harvard. This isn't necessarily a bad thing; I enjoyed my college experience a great deal, as most Harvard students do. But one of the most amazing things about that environment was the way the school operated to instill a very specific sense of social entitlement into each and every student. After I left Harvard, I felt confident that I could enter any environment in the world. I like to think that this confidence has served me well. In some students, of course, the sense of entitlement is excessive, and that became achingly clear to me during the Living Wage Campaign.

For some months before invading and besieging the university president's Massachusetts Hall office in Harvard Yard, a coalition of undergraduate and graduate students had been agitating for what they called a living wage for all of Harvard's employees, including its janitors, food-preparation staff, and landscapers. The issue, as I read it on the posters that appeared all over campus, was that by hiring subcontracting companies that paid workers as little as $8 an hour, the school employed a substantial percentage of these people to do the hardest and dirtiest work on campus for the lowest price possible. Some Harvard students deduced from this fact that living on such a wage did not allow these particular employees—most of whom were Latino, with limited English skills—the opportunity to live in the town where they worked. Living in Cambridge, the students deduced, required a wage of at least $10.25 an hour, and they concluded that a school with the resources to make it one of the largest nonprofit organizations in the world could spare a couple of extra dollars an hour for those who did the thankless work on campus.

On April 18, 2001, nearly fifty members of the Progressive Student Labor Movement invaded university president Neil Rudenstine's office. They remained there for twenty-one days, severely disrupting the school's administrative hierarchy and drawing international attention to its payroll practices. Up until the moment of the invasion I had believed the Living Wage Campaign was just another student protest. And in my opinion, student protests at Harvard—as at most of the other colleges with which I was familiar—had a whiff of resignation about them. The issues for sit-ins and rallies always seemed obscure and limited, a halfhearted attempt by progressive-minded undergraduates to experience some of the euphoria they had heard about from their parents or 1960s-era student activists. The issue, I felt, was just a vehicle around which students could practice gathering, since the number of women or people of color on the tenured faculty, the right of the ROTC to recruit on campus, and the ignorant comments made by a member of the staff are simply not issues with immediate and vital outcomes for the whole of the country. But as students we felt a need to demonstrate about something, and since we had abandoned the fight against an overarching political or social system, satellite problems would have to suffice. In my experience, demonstrations on campus appeared according to a familiar pattern: Whenever a problem presented itself in a form that provoked the prerequisite sense of injury in a substantial group of students, someone would organize a meeting, which led to a protest or rally. Future strategizing meetings took place during dinner in one of Harvard's houses on the river. Occasionally the aggrievement persisted for weeks or months, mostly in the form of discussion groups and letters to the *Harvard Crimson,* but it was usually drained out by the time the reading period for final exams began. As the editor in chief of a magazine that occasionally sponsored protests and rallies, I witnessed many of these mutating controversies, and I must confess that in time I grew weary of righteous indignation that had been scheduled, like everything else in our lives.

So no one was more impressed than I was when members of the Progressive Student Labor Movement began to live their Living Wage Campaign in the fullest and most passionate way, jeopardizing their grades, health, and status at the university in the process. They squatted in President Rudenstine's office just two weeks before the spring reading period was to commence, and as final exams approached it was still unclear whether or not the university was going to negotiate. Some professors agreed to modify their grading plans for the encamped; other professors had less sympathy. As the days dragged on administrators began to speak of oblique punishments for the protesters. It may have been only a threat, but I have little doubt that the notion of expulsion weighed heavily on the demonstrators as the days stretched to weeks and they grew sticky, lethargic, and tense in the quaint, showerless office.

I was moved. For the first time I began to speak with genuine feeling about a campus struggle. Living wages for all employees— a concept that continues to strike me as a necessary practice for an organization with the resources of Harvard University—became my refrain. I wore the buttons. I attended the rallies in front of Massachusetts Hall. I grew impatient with students who questioned our right to stand for the underpaid workers who were, they pointed out, unwilling to risk their livelihoods by invading the president's office or even by speaking up for themselves. The latter point—that the undercompensated workers had failed to stand up for themselves— had never seemed to me to possess any merit. The workers were subcontractors and had very little power when it came to negotiating with the university. Besides, to many Harvard students a real-world job that paid $8 an hour was an insult, but to many of the workers it was a lifeline they could not afford to lose.

Whether or not our protest for them had merit was a question that only surfaced for me when I heard one of those underpaid workers speak for himself at a rally two weeks into the siege.

His name was Santiago, and he worked in one of the campus dining halls. The university had hired him through a subcontracting company, said one of the protest organizers by way of an introduction, and that company paid him $9 an hour.

The organizer handed the bullhorn to Santiago, and I pressed the balls of my feet into the ground so that I might see him over the dozens of people standing in front of me. I caught only a glimpse— brown skin, a short, spare frame, the crimson baseball cap that was part of his uniform settled neatly on his head—and his speech was stammering and broken. But he stood before us with an aura of dignity that was as tentative as it was new, because, he told us, his young daughter had been telling him to stand straight and look people in the eye.

She has been learning these things at school, Santiago said, and while I am so happy that she has the opportunity to be educated in the United States, I do look at the lovely elementary schools in Cambridge and wish that it might be possible for her to attend one of them. I have heard about these schools from my friends. We all work in the dining hall together, and we talk about them during the hour that it takes for us to ride the bus and the subway into Cambridge at four in the morning. Then we talk about them again as we ride out at six o'clock at night. And when I am lucky and there is overtime, I think about these schools as I fall asleep alone on the subway at eleven o'clock at night. My daughter worries about me. She says it is dangerous to fall asleep on the subway. She is right, I know this. And sometimes I worry, too. So I think it would be won- derful if I did not have to ride the subway late at night, and it would be wonderful if she could go to school in Cambridge. She is a smart child. The school she goes to now does not like smart children. I would like her to have a good school that likes smart children. I ask the students in the dining hall where I work about schools. Most of them laugh at me or ignore me, or pretend that they did not hear what I said, though I do talk in English. But a few of them will talk to me, and they told me and my friends that the public schools in Cambridge do great things with smart children. Some of these schools, they told us, even send girls and boys to Harvard.

Santiago paused in his speech, and the crowd began to cheer. I felt confused as the crowd roared and Santiago stared at us with bewilderment. The organizer stepped forward to take the bullhorn, and Santiago shuffled slowly back to join the previous speakers sitting in front of Massachusetts Hall. When he reached his destination, he turned to look at us again. His face was stony, stunned, and unblinking. He stood there frozen as the next speaker, an expert on the university's accounting and budgeting procedures, was introduced. When the man began to speak, I was still watching Santiago, and suddenly I was seized by a sickness that did not pass for the remaining weeks of the siege. When I learned that the university administrators had sat down with the protest organizers and worked out a compromise—a new committee would re-examine the wages of Harvard's lowest-paid workers, and the university issued a moratorium on the practice of subcontracting workers—my illness got worse. I retreated from other people. I spent most of my last two months at Harvard shut away in my room, curled up on the floor, staring silently out at nothing. When I did venture out, it was to get as far away from campus as I could. I was trying to make sense of what it meant for me to have joined a group of people who found it appropriate to disregard the hopes and dreams of a man like Santiago. As the days passed and I refused to appear at any of the senior-year activities, my friends grew concerned. While it was certainly in my plans to attend the graduation ceremony, where we would be receiving our diplomas—while nothing, in fact, could have been more vital to my plans—I began to grow concerned for myself.

So I chose to self-medicate, and the night before graduation I packed up my dorm room, walked out, and proceeded to drink so heavily that remembering anything, even the route I needed to walk home, proved elusive. When I collapsed in bed that night, Santiago had faded from my mind. I slept heavily and awoke with a small smile on my face.

I also awoke late. When I look back on it, I believe it was part of my secret intention. If I awoke late, I would be forced to hurry. If I were forced to hurry, I would be too busy to remember.

I did not have time for a shower or meticulous grooming. I opened a new bottle of infant-rehydration formula and drank half of it. Then I slipped my gown over my head and pinned on my cap. At the last moment I remembered the high probability of pictures, so I grabbed a tube of lipstick from my dresser. As I snatched it I snagged my thumb on the Living Wage badge I had turned face-down next to it, and it was then that Santiago came back to me with a shudder.

Where was he? I wondered as I picked up the badge and pinned it to my gown. I wondered if he was working overtime at one of the houses on the river to prepare the brunch we would eat after the ceremony. I wondered if he had heard about the compromise and whether it would provide enough for his family to achieve the hopes he had for them. I wondered what he thought of it and whether or not he would be one of the affected workers. I wondered if it would be enough, if he would be able to move his family into a community that had good schools and liked smart children. I had seen with my own family how much that dream would cost.

For weeks I had done everything possible to avoid these thoughts. But as I marched to my graduation ceremony with Santiago on my mind I felt a numbing sense of relief. I did not know if he would have what he needed to pass his dreams on to his family. I did not know if that even mattered, since he had to live in a world where the most privileged of all students laughed at his dreams. I did not know if I could do anything about it, but I did know that I had to try, because I had seen his stony, stunned, unblinking stare before, and I knew that it was a call for my indictment.

I had been called to account for Santiago, just as I had been called to account for George on the afternoon of my high school graduation, at a reception at my family's house. I had not wanted a reception after the graduation ceremony. The inherent egotism of throwing a party for oneself makes me uncomfortable; I do not enjoy self-promotion, despite what the testament of this document suggests to the contrary. I wanted to receive my diploma by mail. When it appeared that I would be expected to attend the reception, I called Lila and George in a panic.

It was no use. Neither of them felt comfortable among the throng of family, family friends, and associates who filled the back-yard. My parents socialize with the same horrified infrequency as I do, so I did not know even the names of some of the guests. What I did know—and I knew this from the stiff, labored way in which they carried and presented themselves—was that most of them had fought their way to a position of respectability from modest or impoverished means. The cost of performing such a Herculean task is incalculable, and one of the side effects can be reduced tolerance for those who have not made the same choices with their lives. I felt the burden of that scrutiny as the guest of honor, so I imagine that it was certainly present for my friends. It may have been part of the reason why Lila opted to leave early and come back to fetch me in the evening—she and I were planning a drive up to San Francisco to buy drugs and seek out mischief. It was certainly part of the reason why George disappeared during the afternoon. I felt his absence immediately, but it was more than an hour after his retreat before I had a break in which to search for him. I slipped away from accepting congratulations and answering questions about achievements for which I harbored my doubts, and I tore through the front yard and the house looking for my friend. At last I spotted him in the living room. He stood alone in front of the window, and as I approached I saw that he had drawn the curtains open so that he might look out on the party on the patio. His head was ducked to the side. His spine was curled in on itself; his hands were in his pockets; and as he turned to confront his visitor I saw for the first time the well-dressed, respectable guests, I heard the gentle clink of wineglasses and the gurgle of the pool filter, and as I careered to a halt before his picture window I felt the fact of my education, the sun-dappled appearance of my life, and the weight of my privilege for the first time. He stared at me in silence. Then, slowly, he turned back to stare at the party. I turned to look with him. We did not speak.

As we stood there it occurred to me that George was only twenty years old and that despite the depth of his life experience there were yet a few things that he did not recognize. It occurred to me in the same instant that the Youth Outlook community to which George and I had belonged may have looked vastly different to him than it had to me, and that his response to its breakdown might not have been sorrow; but those thoughts upset me so much that I pushed them away. I still needed to believe in strange concepts like authenticity and the moral superiority of struggle, and I could not do that if I imagined George's desire for my life.

I have different beliefs now. Some of the change has come with age and experience, some has come from the wisdom of others. But most of it comes from the fact that I now live in Potrero Hill, where at tremendous financial strain I bought a home close to San Francisco General Hospital. I spend most of my days fretting about mortgage payments and the real estate market and the rough, angry children who stand in front of my house while they wait for the bus to Hunters Point, but sometimes, late at night, I hear the keen of an ambulance and I wake with a start. It's George I'm worrying about on those nights. And the worry does not leave me until I remember that he would want me to make a home for my family in San Francisco, and that he will not be coming to San Francisco General Hospital anymore.

CHAPTER FIVE

ALL MY LIFE I have made demands of California.

I asked for the experience of my own authentic culture, and I found Guillermo and St. Augustine's Church.

I asked for an education, and I found Bret Harte and an identity narrative of my own design.

I asked for the experience of community, of homes and families, and I found Hans and his cousin, George and his father.

I asked California to provide a home for me as it had for my parents. This was more complicated.

After I graduated from Harvard, I moved into an apartment in Brooklyn and a job in New York City. I knew only that I wanted the experience of living in New York; I don't know what I expected my life to be like there. Certainly I hoped to expunge myself of any remaining tinge of San Jose provinciality and perhaps acquire certain urbane and sophisticated ways. But I underestimated the toll that a place like New York City can have on a person of my temperament. I am prone to excess under the best of conditions; in New York I felt myself all too quickly developing the status obsession and bitter sense of want that flourishes in the city's compact spaces. Most troubling was the sense of isolation I felt while I was living there; I did not understand my own desires and could not comprehend why I felt so hungry. I was hungry to achieve some sort of satiation; to achieve anything. Some nights I felt so starved that I acted out. I can remember screaming matches with strangers in bars on the Lower East Side of Manhattan—and trudging home from the subway station at three o'clock one morning, turning around to see a strange man following me, and feeling numb (I did not know him, nor had I invited him to join me, but I faced the possibility of violence with indifference, even relief)—and I shudder. I didn't know who I was during those months. I'm a bit better acquainted with that person now, and feel a bit more sympathy for her plight. I was looking for New York to provide me with what I thought I had been denied in California. Of course it was hopeless.

When my roommate was killed in the September 11 attacks, I spent the first three days crying. After that I turned off the television and tried to summon up memories to honor the dead man. I remembered, for instance, how quickly we would drop whatever we were doing to dance and sing along to the silliest pop songs we found on the radio. And I remembered my fight with our kitchen stove, which needed to be lit with a match. The procedure involved deep knee bends, a great deal of hand-eye coordination, and the risk of scorched fingertips and eyebrows. I was too intimidated to try it, so I asked him constantly, and every time he lit the stove without complaining. I walked into his bedroom to find more memories. He had hung a poster of the World Trade Center above his bed. He loved working there.

With the television off I found a sense of quiet within the city that allowed me to take stock of certain facts. There was the fact that I was being pushed out of my apartment, for instance—our lease was up, and our landlord was sensitive to the neighborhood's new bistros and Pilates studios that had filled me with such malice. He had presented us with a substantial rent increase, and I had already begun packing up. Then there was the fact that some months previous I had used a temporary fit of self-awareness to apply for a small grant from the Ella Lyman Cabot Trust, and I had just received word that the grant would be funded. Most of all, there was the fact of my roommate's death, and the death of thousands with him, and all of the noise and tragedy that was sure to follow.

I bought an airplane ticket to Johannesburg. I had one laptop computer, two suitcases, and three e-mail addresses for acquaintances who claimed that they would be of assistance to me upon my arrival. When the moment came, only one of them responded. His name was Tom Masland. He was the supremely capable and appealingly insouciant Africa bureau chief for *Newsweek* magazine. When we met in Cape Town, he asked me what I was doing in South Africa.

Are you on the run from something? he said. I don't mean that in a bad way, because of course we all are. But I'd like to know.

In response I told him about the first time I had come to South Africa, about how my heart had swelled in my throat when the plane touched down at Johannesburg International Airport and from the window I saw the waist-high veld, grown all the way up to the tarmac and bending under the wind with a satiny glow. I told him about the six weeks I had spent in Pretoria working as a student intern for a human rights law firm. I had heard countless stories of atrocity, but I still walked home every night and wiped the red, red dust from my shoes with a feeling of awe and amazement. I told him how it had felt to live in a country unafraid and unashamed to live with its own history, despite the horror that entailed. And I told him that I didn't know what I was doing, but I had a feeling that such a place might have something to teach me. Tom listened patiently, then he asked me how I was getting by in South Africa this time around. I lobbed off some cheerful, lighthearted answer, with which I may have even succeeded in convincing him had he not witnessed my departure: Our meeting was the occasion of one of my first attempts to maneuver a right-side car with a manual transmission. To this day I believe it was this ridiculous display, and not my education or experience, that earned me my first freelance assignment for Tom.

As time passed I came to consider Tom my second father. He was the best of role models: a man who had covered the world's most dangerous places (Beirut, Tehran, Mozambique, Madagascar, Mogadishu) for decades while still managing to devote himself to his family. He never drew attention to his talents or achievements. He never even drew attention to things that would have been life-defining for other people. (Oh, it's just fine, he told me after I contacted him in a panic over an international news report that he had been injured by shrapnel in Liberia. They stitched me right up. Just a couple of nicks to the arm.) To him, risk was as regular and necessary as every other aspect of life, and I only began to appreciate this after I had written a few stories for him. Each of my attempts was more passable than the previous one, and it began to dawn on me that Tom believed that it lay within the realm of possibility for me to assume the glamorous title of freelance journalist in and around southern Africa. I never completely believed it myself, even while I was living it. Maybe that is why I ran off with the Englishman.

When I met the Englishman, he was the owner of a London-based art-direction company. This profession occupied him sixteen hours a day, often seven days a week, in the many different countries that are used as cheap, colorful backdrops in film. He earned an excellent living and had very little time for other things. For those reasons and many more he indulged in frequent and bemused recollections of his previous existence as a sculptor. On the night we met he presented the following summary of his career: When I was doing nothing but my sculpture, I had no money and all the time in the world. I had endless hours for everything else in my life, endless hours, because it was mentally and psychologically excruciating to work on my own sculpture for more than a few hours a day. Each day, when I could not bring myself to do any more, when I had given up on the silly hope that I might be able to wrestle meaning out of my material—whether it was clay, stone, steel, dung, or rough-hewn wood, it didn't matter; I tried them all—I paced in my studio or spent hours examining what I had done. I suppose I was hoping that my pitiful offering might give me a moment of brilliance. Of course it would always go pear-shaped, and I walked away feeling exhausted and terrified. I don't know how I was able to face the idea of going back in the morning. Each night when I left the studio I was a defeated man. But I always came back. Again and again. In the morning I woke up full of determination. Or spite, or resignation, something. Each morning I woke up full of some rubbish that forced me to march into my studio determined to see the project out to its catastrophic end. And it always was catastrophic in my eyes. I'll never create anything as lovely as the things I envision.

At any rate, I might have gone on like that forever, he said. But one day I decided that I should take up some work. I went to a foundry that I had often passed with a strange feeling of longing. I opened the door. There was a young man at the front, a short man with coppery hair and broken teeth and clay-spattered coveralls, and when I had stood there staring for far too long he snapped at me, Well, what do you want, then? And I told him in my poshest public school accent that I was desirous of employment. Then it was his turn to stare. His name was Robby. I worked with him for two years. I came to admire him. I came to admire many of the men who worked in the foundry. I learned more about what it meant to be a workingman at that foundry than I learned about sculpture. I mean, really. All I learned about sculpture was that most people who buy it only want tits and tails—a nude woman or a baby deer for their bloody back garden. I came away feeling that it was far more important that I had learned real respect for the workingman. And I don't mean some sort of cheap sentiment, either. I mean that I understood how profound it is to spend your entire life doing hard physical work for wealthy people who have no bloody recognition of the toll it takes. The foundry was exhausting and it was relentless and there was no reward but the pub after quitting time. Once I made some sense of all this, about the way my co-workers' lives were moving in these horrible circles, I realized that my years in the foundry were more valuable than any other experience I could imagine. Especially the sorts of experiences that my classmates described as better fits for men of our station.

The matter of station was a curious one for the Englishman. He came from a well-to-do family in one of London's best neighborhoods. By British standards, standards that are exact on nothing but gauging another's social standing, he came from a family that could boast of a good deal of status—nothing exceptional, but solid claims to good taste and gentility. The interesting fact was that his family was exceptional indeed in their home country of Poland. Prior to the Second World War, the Englishman's parents were born into a tradition that in some ways had remained unchanged since feudalism. They learned, as children, that there were strict codes of behavior by which nobles were expected to abide; they learned, too, that in due time they would be expected to assume the duties and dignities of their rank. Castles, estates, titles, public responsibilities—all these should have been theirs. But what had survived the Industrial Age and the scourges of modernity fell to Hitler's army, and the Englishman's parents abandoned the gains of their forebears in exchange for base survival. One of them reached England nestled in a corner of her mother's coat, the other aboard one of the famous *Kindertransports* by which desperate parents in occupied areas consigned their children to unknown futures. Neither of his parents could tally much of the past beyond abysmal loss. Their families were ruined and rootless. Many of their relatives had been lost—to concentration camps, to

battles, to despair. They began again in London and, all circumstances notwithstanding, did quite well for themselves. If I noticed the
burden of history's weight on them at all when I met them later in
London, it was only in the small and inexplicable pauses in conversation, the avoidance of eye contact during their presentation of even
the most innocuous stories, the sudden menace that could surface at
any moment in jovial bickering over a family meal.

And perhaps it had come through in their children, the way history often does. I asked the Englishman more than once how his
family's history had affected him. He replied with a sense of surety
that it had not. I'm an Englishman as far as I'm concerned, he said. I
don't even speak Polish. Not that I'm in denial of anything, certainly
I'm not. I'm quite proud of my family and of what we've gotten
through. And of course it's quite nice to have a name that'll get you
a table in Poland. But has it affected me, the way I see myself, the
way I see my life? No, not a bit. I want to make art and be with my
friends and live in the country. That's good old bloody old England
through and through.

And he did indeed want, with an energetic ardor that was
moving, to simply make his art and be with his friends and live in the
country. The first time he told me this I was twenty-three years old
and we were winding our way through South Africa and up the
coast of Mozambique. It was early autumn. The temperature held
steady at eighty-five degrees, the sky was big, and the sea was the
color of lilacs. When I flew over the ocean off the Mozambican coast
in a microlight plane I could see whale sharks from a thousand
feet. I could see, too, if I dared to close my eyes for a moment, the

palm-sized prawns I would eat for dinner that night. The prawns would come to me out of my vision, grilled with peri-peri sauce and butter, and we would eat them while the electricity failed and we coated ourselves with mosquito repellent. In Mozambique we slept in huts on cots draped with netting, and we rambled about in a 1963 Land Rover with a bad clutch and a gearshift that was missing its grip. In South Africa we ate fresh yellowtail and spent nights at Clifton Beach while young men who were teaching themselves to spin flaming poi practiced near our camp. I was falling in love with a man who had, I thought, refused to surrender the childish determination that he could build himself a better world. And because of that, I began to sense my own possibilities in a way that I never had.

The second time he told me about how he saw his life we were in a warehouse in east London and I was crying. He told me all of it again—It simply has to be, he said. Life in London leaves you so knackered that you can't remember why you wanted to make art in the first place. That's why I want to live in the country, in a place like Northumberland, where it's green and quiet. And I keep thinking about a big stone house. Even though they get cold in the winter there's fireplaces and all sorts of fantastic things you can do with heating now. Something big enough for all the friends and children and dogs. Something so that life is possible, so that art is possible. That's why I'm working so hard right now. So that it can be. And here he stopped, and I sobbed harder, because he had not added the last line I remembered from the first speech (*And so that you can be with me*) and because I knew that he never would again. We were falling apart, and he had lost faith that we could bring things back together, because that was what his own history had taught him, and of course he was right.

That night we went to his parents' home for dinner. That was the midsummer's evening when the Englishman's father, for whom I felt great fondness, showed me his exquisite back garden and in return I tried to seize him by the throat. Dinner had gone poorly. The Englishman was miserable and brooding and I was miserable and quiet. His sisters had kept up appearances with a constant flow of chatter, but there was an air of resignation about their efforts; an acceptance that they could do only so much. His parents were pre-occupied with thoughts of which only they were aware, though this did not stop father and son from breaking into an uncomfortable, ill-tempered spat. I'm sure everyone was relieved when the dessert dishes were cleared and the party broke up into separate rooms—mother to the kitchen, siblings to the living room, the Englishman to wander about the house in a silent fury. His father stayed outside to drink a Scotch in the garden. I wanted to be as inconspicuous as possible, so I tiptoed to the back window, where I hoped I could admire the garden in peace. Soon, though, the Englishman's father glanced up and noticed me. With a cock of his head, he motioned for me to join him.

I walked out onto the patio. Side by side, we admired the family's handiwork: the lush, neatly trimmed yard, the elegant low bushes, the massive rose trellis that served as its focal point. The Englishman's father sipped his Scotch and winked at me. Not bad, eh? he said. The ice cubes tinkled in his tumbler. I strained to hear over them as he began to speak, shyly at first, then with strength and vigor, about the garden. I love to garden, and I work very hard at it, he said. Because I didn't always think I was great with a plant. I've always had ideas, of course. We knew we wanted something simple and well planned, not in the classic style of an English garden. No tangles of hollyhock, no whirls of cyclamen. No overgrown flower beds and bloody bushes everywhere mucking everything up. And for God's sake no crawling ivy—something simple. So we worked on this garden for twenty years, and this is what we have to show for it. He stopped abruptly and stared blankly into the garden. And it was just at that moment—as he stood there with the summer stars soft on his shoulders and his Scotch tumbler tinkled and he stared with a calm dead look on his face—it was just at that moment that I was overcome. In one jerky movement I thrust my hands forward and pulled them back. And he saw me. He must have seen me. At the very least he must have seen, and recognized, the flush of emotion rising up my chest and into my throat, because it felt very clear to me in the moment that I grabbed my own wrists that I didn't need to hear about his lovely garden. Nor did I need to hear his opinions on classic English landscaping. Though I found these comments interesting, it was the last time I would be in his house. I knew it and he knew it. I felt that he needed to tell me something else.

He needed to tell me what he had felt on the cold gray day he stood on a quay in a long line of quivering children. He would have dug his small white fists deep into his pockets, and as he stared, blinking, into the flat granite sky he would have told himself that it was all right, that the tears in his eyes came only from having his scarf wound about his neck so tightly and his coat buttons fastened so snugly. Perhaps with these thoughts of the immediate he had banished it all—all of what he felt as he waited for the ship to deliver him to England from Brittany or Bratislava or the Hook of Holland, wherever they were (he might not have known; he might have been so overwhelmed by the circumstances under which he left Warsaw and so concerned with the unimaginable responsibility of caring for himself that the exact location didn't figure into his consciousness). Perhaps he had to. I have never been in his moment. I have never been a seven-year-old boy who had once been heir to his people and was now alone on a quay, stripped, heir to nothing but a small leather suitcase and the future he would build in a country of which he knew not even the language. So I don't know what he could have kept of his feelings or of his country. I don't even know if it is possible for anything to remain. But if it is possible, then I need to know. I need to know what he kept, and in the moment that my hands flew up I needed to know quite badly. I was overcome by my grief at losing his son. I needed to rebuild my life, and I didn't know what to value in this new one. He had survived losses that were beyond my comprehension. I felt that he had learned something about what to do in the face of loss, what to hold on to when rebuilding, and I knew it wasn't rose trellises and French oak furniture and dinner parties in the back garden in summer. If I knew what he had kept, then I would know what I should carry, what we all should carry, as we wander through the history of our lives.

But he didn't tell me. Perhaps he held on to nothing, or perhaps he felt that I should find the answers for myself. Perhaps he felt that my needs overstepped the boundaries of propriety, which they surely did, or perhaps he had not yet discovered what he had kept.

That may be why he responded the way he did: He stared at me with kindness, and the most peculiar sense of outrage. Then he turned away from me and walked into his house.

I left England a few days after that.

I went back to Cape Town. I moved into an azalea-colored house in the Bo-Kaap neighborhood, and I tried to create the answers for myself. There, in the Bo-Kaap, I found magic rather than answers, and it's important for me to mention that I don't use the word *magic* in jest. I am a skeptic and a Jamesian pragmatist, so while I believe that magic exists, I'm more apt to look for rational explanations. I looked—and the fact remains that the Bo-Kaap is a magical place. It doesn't resemble any other part of Cape Town. There are 947 houses and 5,000 residents. The tightly packed homes are painted in outrageous shades of chartreuse and fuchsia and periwinkle and mango. The entire neighborhood resembles a postcard replica of tourist areas in Morocco or Tunisia or Zanzibar or even Indonesia, which most of the residents draw some of their heritage from and possess a distinct longing for, for no other reason than that they presume a respect for their Islamic religion exists there that is unfathomable in South Africa. This longing for faraway lands extends to every aspect of the neighborhood. The residents have done their best to transform the city's best examples of eighteenth- and nineteenth-century Dutch-Georgian architecture into *riads*. The homes are linked by narrow cobbled streets and open-plan courtyards. The whitewashed steps leading from house to house are crumbling; the stone fountains in the courtyards sputter with age. The houses are linked by all these physical features, but above all, they are linked by the mosques—nine in all—which operate at all hours and exert a strange and omnipotent influence over the neighborhood.

The residents believe that those mosques saved the Bo-Kaap during apartheid: While every urban neighborhood that was inhabited by mixed-race (or colored) people was being demolished by the government both in Cape Town and all over the country, the Bo-Kaap was allowed to stand. There is no logical reason for this. The Bo-Kaap has the best weather in Cape Town. It is historic, it is picturesque, and it is conveniently located next to the city center. District Six, the sprawling colored neighborhood to the west of the city center, was razed and flattened in the 1960s. Colored families were forcibly removed from Rondebosch, from Rosebank, from Claremont. And yet the Bo-Kaap remains.

The residents believe that the apartheid government dared not remove the nine mosques in their community. They told me this with such ferocity that I realized they believe the mosques will protect them from all disturbances to come. I hope that they are right, for this is what they have to protect in the Bo-Kaap: The sight of young couples strolling hand-in-hand at dusk. The children, far too many to count, who lord over street traffic all day and night with games of cricket and pickup soccer. The imams who gather on street corners after evening prayers, arguing theological points and slapping one another on the back with copies of the Koran. The way the smell of a good curry draws all the neighbors over to share. The dawn call from the muezzin, the afternoon roar from the fish hawker, and the evening jazz from the ice-cream truck. The way older women shuttle among one another's homes, giggling, so that they might share tea and gossip while they mend clothes—for in the Bo-Kaap, clothes are mended rather than thrown out. The residents must protect these things. Above all they must protect the safety they have established through their tightly knit community: The Bo-Kaap is the only neighborhood in Cape Town where young women feel comfortable walking alone at night—despite the neighborhood's forty percent unemployment rate, despite its homeless population, despite its gangs. This is what makes the neighborhood's magic possible, and it is certainly possible every day. I know because it made my life possible. When I moved to the Bo-Kaap, I was in such a state that I found it impossible to believe in anything. But as I began to walk the sun-drenched streets of my new home, and as I began to see what the Bo-Kaap had protected despite overwhelming odds, I imagined that if the Bo-Kaap could remain, then perhaps I would endure as well.

That's how it began. I had only wanted to show gratitude. I had only wanted, in fact, to save the Bo-Kaap. The neighborhood was in danger again, and this time the enemy was insidious. The transformation of government had affected the neighborhood in new and unexpected ways. Economics were accomplishing a turnover of a community that even apartheid had failed to shake.

Architecture and graphic-design firms were buying the largest homes on the perimeter of the business district; the new owners demolished the high stoops and the old Dutch windows and rebuilt their spaces as steel-and-glass aviaries. Prices for new lots and old homes were skyrocketing. According to local newspapers, during a six-month period in 2002–2003 the price of a two-bedroom house in the central Bo-Kaap rose by 400,000 rand. And with an economic shift came a demographic shift. On my evening strolls I saw more and more fashionable young people hosting loud *braais* and cocktail parties on their roofs while the muezzins wailed and our neighbors, swathed in white from head to toe as though they were wrapped in shrouds, ran to mosque.

For the first time I recognized, with a sense of dread, that I was a part of the neighborhood's demise. I knew, too, that any solo attempt to stop the steamroll of a market-based economy would be an exercise in futility—I had learned that well enough from the Bay Area. So I chose a task where I believed I could be successful: demanding compensation from the film companies that had decided the Bo-Kaap was *the* new place to shoot.

Approximately once a week, film companies and photography agencies shut down the main corridors of the neighborhood: Upper Wale, Chiappini, and Rose streets. They often didn't shut down these streets officially, which would have required clearance from city officials, but swept in on the day of the shoot with their own cones, signs, and armed security to declare the area closed. I spoke to the staff on these shoots in the hope of getting information about how they planned to compensate residents for the hassle and the use of their faces and property. (Passing residents were occasionally encouraged to stand in front of their homes, or some other location designated by the director, to add local color to the images.) The conversations were uncomfortable and laborious, the staff easily offended, and I always left feeling as though I had been extraordinarily presumptuous to ask questions. In time, this feeling morphed into a slow-burning anger, and I abandoned myself to the activity of which I'm most skeptical: political activism. The only outcome of this that proved even remotely positive was my friendship with Keith.

We met at a Bo-Kaap community meeting. The purpose of the meeting was presumably community outreach and data distribution for a real estate development company that had recently purchased a prime lot on the slopes of Signal Hill. I don't believe the developers expected to meet 250 grim faces when they walked into the neighborhood meeting hall. But there we were, and we were unimpressed with their sputtered greetings and the transparencies they displayed on the overhead projector they had brought in from their office downtown. As quickly as they could, the developers shared their ideas for the lot they had purchased, most of which involved building an abominable formation of condominiums that would overlook the heart of the neighborhood. Then they turned over the podium to their audience, which consisted exclusively of local matrons and patriarchs over the age of forty, and me. I considered standing up to speak, but I was not certain that I had anything constructive to suggest for the developers to consider when building on their lot. As it happened, neither did anyone else.

The evening evolved into an elaboration of neighborhood needs by a growing list of malcontents. Many of them, I'm sure, weren't even aware of the extent of their dissatisfaction until they heard their neighbors articulate complaints. I watched with amusement as the demands piled up—better schools and more adult educational opportunities, reliable refuse collection, activities for youth and teenagers, employment, employment, and employment—and the development representatives shriveled in their chairs. As the list of speakers grew, the content of their presentations became increasingly dramatic, and soon the audience felt inclined toward participation with applause, cheers, and commentary. I was entertained, but I didn't believe that anything of substance would be accomplished by such an extravagant display of the neighborhood's resentments toward governmental and private entities that were unrelated to the people who had organized this meeting. I was thinking about making my exit when Keith stood up to speak.

Keith was a copper-colored man in his early forties. His body was trim and his limbs were overgrown, so his head, with its towering crown of sculptured black curls, looked like a pecan on the end of a straw. He had a boyish face and brown eyes that expanded to twice their size when he was excited, which was often. When he moved, he appeared to be executing a series of comic contortions. He was also one of the most commanding public speakers I had ever watched.

My fellow Bo-Kaap residents, he said, I would like to address my words to you. Perhaps you have already noticed that your worries and your fears are not being heard by those who are in a position to bring better schools and greater employment to this area. This is a tremendous lapse of integrity on the part of those who are responsible, and I have no answer for their failure. But let me be the first to inform you that neither will you receive any answers from the men and women sitting in front of you with their clipboards and their data sheets about the length of time for construction. Their concern is to be sure that they will have no trouble building their new property. They're not concerned about the problems we're facing on a daily basis. In any case, you cannot expect them to be able to do much about the local educational system, and they certainly do not have any interest in our employment troubles, since the clientele they will be serving will already have substantial incomes. Please understand that they consider this meeting a formality. Possibly they consider themselves generous for asking for our input in the first place. And perhaps they should, since I have observed that this is not the kind of neighborhood that issues complaints when others move in to take advantage. That is our failure, and that is what I wish to speak to you about tonight. Some of you may have noticed that there is a great deal of construction going on in the Bo-Kaap. Some others may have noticed the increasing number of tourists and video companies crowding into the Bo-Kaap; you have no choice but to notice if you live on Upper Wale or Chiappini or one of the other streets these buses and photo shoots love to invade. And there may be a few of you who have noticed that the cost of living in the Bo-Kaap is steadily rising with each passing day. Now. For those of you who have noticed one or perhaps all of these things, I would like to ask you what you have done about it. Have you taken a moment, on your stoop during a hot night, to share your opinion with your neighbor? What have you done beyond this? Have you considered how all of those things are related? I would challenge you to consider the fact that they are, and I would further challenge you to consider the fact that if you are concerned with education and employment in the Bo-Kaap, then you will have to come up against the other activities taking place here. For these other things are draining the neighborhood of resources and attention. And until we as a community address what we wish to demand from those who would walk into our neighborhood and take advantage of what we have built here, no community meeting and no condominium builder is going to make any difference.

A long moment of silence followed Keith's speech. The quiet was broken only by a quick tapping noise as one of the development representatives ticked a pen against his clipboard.

After the meeting was adjourned I searched for Keith. The crowd was older and slower and still grumbling about the problems they hadn't even been aware that they had, so it took time for me to find him. He was standing alone at the back of the room. I gripped his hand and introduced myself. Then I told him that I was willing to take up his challenge, for I had indeed noticed the increasing incidence of all those things and I wished to do something about it. He did not seem at all surprised at anything about me or my declaration. I am pleased that the charms of the Bo-Kaap have reached as far away as California, he said. Perhaps when you return there, you can inform the Californians about how we live here. Please remember to tell them of the pride and not just the poverty.

Keith was to make me aware of nearly everything I know about how we lived in the Bo-Kaap, and how we in the Bo-Kaap lived in South Africa. By rights he was a strange choice of teacher: He had spent most of his adult life in exile. As a teenager he became a student activist with a fledgling branch of the African National Congress in Cape Town. Within a couple of years the government located him, and he fled to the Netherlands. He spent the following twenty years in Amsterdam. I made the mistake of treating my exile as though it were a brief and temporary moment in my life, Keith said. The months away from home became years, and it grew more and more clear that apartheid was not going to crumble and fall away as easily as my youth. I was so attached to the idea of making my home in a free version of my country that I never allowed myself to accept the fact that the Netherlands, which I hated for so long, was as much my home as South Africa ever was and ever will be. At a certain point, he said, I realized that I had to settle into the Netherlands in order to make peace with the fact that I was there, but even my attempts to do that failed. I carry a Dutch passport, and I'm the father of a young woman who does not envision any home for herself but Europe. But when the African National Congress came to power, I was still as rootless and restless as I had been as a student organizer. So I made the psychological leap of returning to a country that I no longer recognize, and now I find myself in the absurd position of living out my teenage dream. I do my best. I live the life of an anonymous citizen. There is little employment here, so I have launched my own business, and in time I hope to employ others. That may be the greatest thing I can do for my country right now. I chose to live in the Bo-Kaap because I did not grow up there, and because it is far away from the colored township in which my family still lives. One of the things that has not changed is our relationship, despite my wish that twenty years might alter our feelings. So I live in the Bo-Kaap, and I work, and I read the newspaper in a fruitless endeavor to educate myself on the current state of this country. I no longer seek out the limelight, and I do not speak in public when I can restrain myself. It really is best for me to stay silent, he said.

I too felt as though every home I tried to make was a fruitless endeavor, but I could not place the blame for that on the politics of my country of birth or my country of residence, and I resented Keith for possessing the luxury of an explanation. We were immediately inseparable and explosively combative. For months the best way for our friends to locate us at any hour of the day or night was to wander the streets of the Bo-Kaap and central Cape Town until they stumbled on the unusual spectacle of two slim, brown figures stumbling and bumbling and arguing about obscure literary or historical points, the efficacy of drug use, and our life stories. We argued about everything, especially when we were in agreement. But when he spoke about the politics of the country in which we were both living, in a state of high bewilderment, I fell quiet to let him speak his advice to me:

In your country you may be called black, he said, but in this country you are colored, and it may be to your advantage to learn the behavior expected of you as a colored woman. It will be difficult in some ways. You do not share the accent, the language, the religion, the culture, or the history of South Africa's colored people. Your facial features are not even similar to ours. But none of that will make a tremendous difference, provided that you understand how to act in such a manner as to make others feel comfortable and secure in their understanding of the place colored people occupy in this country. If you are interested in a peaceful existence with marginal security, it is crucial that you can live within other people's expectations. That is one of the most useful lessons I can pass on to you. It is as wretched as it sounds, and you must disregard it whenever you can, but there are times when it may be necessary for your safety. So when that time comes, the first observance you will be expected to adopt is a stubborn and subterranean disgust for the black people of this country. Do not neglect to call them blacks, either, or Africans, as if those terms were something strange to you. Considering that we now have a black government and a new set of rules to live by, you must adopt this attitude in a subtle manner, but not so subtle that black people believe you see them as equals. Express the true force of your manufactured venom only in colored company. You should behave as though whites are not to be trusted, but if you can bear it, you might want to consider dating one. Dating one does not indicate that you trust them as a group. Besides, many white men love the exoticism of colored women, and if you are clever you can demand quite a bit from them. I would encourage you to view your choice of male company as an opportunity to express your political beliefs, since that is how others will analyze it. A colored boyfriend is the safest and most acceptable companion, but a white boyfriend can be a status symbol in certain colored communities. In their eyes, a white boyfriend means not only that you fit the most stringent standards of mainstream beauty, but also that you'll have the possibility of a baby with light skin, straight hair, and better financial prospects abroad. However, if you desire to send the opposite message, you should date a black man. A black boyfriend sends the message that you hold yourself above the narrow politics of the colored community as well as the entitlement of whites. He would be a way to establish your solidarity with the current establishment of this country and a vehicle by which you might reject the ingrained customs of your ancestors. There are other ways you can express those sentiments, of course, but you are colored and you are a woman and the most powerful understanding this society has of you is in your relationships with men.

That conversation served as a powerful motivation for me to launch my full-scale crusade for the Bo-Kaap. If those were society's general sentiments, then I would rather have done anything but let them judge me accordingly. Far better, I thought, to let them judge me based on my willingness to be proactive in a public fight for a neighborhood, not a public fight for sexual status.

I asked Keith if he would be willing to instruct me in the arts of political organization and public speaking. To my surprise, he offered to join me. In time I came to see that Keith gained a certain relief from engaging in the familiar territory of political struggle, even through a marginal route like the one I had to offer. It is all one and the same, he said when I asked him if the techniques he once used to inspire people with the idea of a free South Africa might work for my vision of a respected and preserved Bo-Kaap. We will treat this neighborhood as we would treat an incoming class of students, or a group of wealthy housewives in Rotterdam, or a bar full of unemployed miners in Johannesburg. We may modulate the message, but we will use the same strategy. And you will see that it is all the same struggle.

So many of Keith's words come back to me now at strange times. I have no idea why we took it upon ourselves to save the Bo-Kaap. Neither of us had a history in the neighborhood. Neither of us shared an abiding love for many elements of the culture that sustained it—

a culture that encouraged silence, especially political silence; a culture where the sole focus was on the tribulations of the extended family. Keith and I are Westerners and to us this way of life is like a remote piece of some ancient past. And yet this past is atavistic, because one afternoon as we sat in my bedroom translating land-use documents, Keith spoke the words that had been buried in the recesses of my consciousness: After so many long nights spent thrashing about in a state of anxiety I have awoken in the Bo-Kaap to find the sun pooling on my face, he said. And the warm nuzzle of the sun has been enough to calm me so that I might hear the sleepy moan of the muezzin and then rouse myself toward the window, where I watch the solid rolling sway of older women carrying baskets of bread or fish for the family meal. The children trip over the hems of their long dresses, and they shoo them away with their free hands, and I can still hear their gossip and their laughter long after they have disappeared into their homes. Only when they have been gone for a long time can I then rise from the window to face my day, and as I do so I ask myself why I have chosen to make my life an interminable struggle.

The people in the Bo-Kaap had built something worth saving. I was never certain whether Keith and I could overcome our own limitations in order to do any saving, but we knew enough to try. Keith advised me on tactics, and I performed the maneuvers. I spent several days in libraries and record offices, tracking down legal codes for the types of land-use and privacy invasions that I believed were taking place. Given the burdens on that country's judicial system, it was unlikely that these disputes would ever be heard before a court of law. I noted them anyway. Your first goal is simply to raise aware-ness of these issues, Keith said. Do not attempt to drive all these foreign film companies out of the Bo-Kaap immediately. Such haste would put you in an awkward position, and it may not be necessary. People modify their own behavior if they believe they are being observed. Remember that as you move through the first stages of this campaign. Observe, inform, and only then should you execute.

For me the joy was in the act of gathering the facts; I did not anticipate actually fulfilling the next stage in Keith's strategy by speaking to my neighbors. I pleaded with Keith to assume responsi-bility for the door-to-door informational segment of our program, but he insisted that I do it. He suggested that I select a familiar face for my first attempt at persuasion, and that is how I found myself standing in front of the elderly woman who lived across the street from me, with my knees quivering and the conversation in my mind alternating between an examination of my grudge against Keith and a rehearsal of the shifts in tonal inflection he had recommended for maximum seduction.

My neighbor's name was Salayla. I met her during my first week in the Bo-Kaap, when she shuffled over to inquire about the strange men she had seen walking in and out of my house. Once contented with my explanation about the furniture haulers, she proceeded to conduct a thorough investigation of my history and background. After such an isolating sojourn in London, I found her endearing. I would often stop by her house on my evening walks around the neighborhood. She would be pondering the movements of the neigh-borhood from behind her living room curtains, and if she had a curry on the stove, she would spoon a few bites into a chipped teacup for me to sample. We would speak of small things, and I would take my curry in sips so as to remain in her presence for that many more seconds. It is not hard to make, she said of the curry. You must come over some afternoon; I will teach you.

I did come over one afternoon, but the purpose of my visit was not the cooking lesson I so dearly desired. She joined me on her stoop while we talked, and at first I allowed myself to imagine that the conversation was going well. She smiled when I began my speech—a miracle in and of itself, since it must be contrary to our innate human capacities to smile at any discussion that opens with the words I spoke to her: I have come to speak to you about the exploitation of your community.

I pressed on with my agenda, recounting all the offenses with the stern expression Keith recommended, and then Salayla interrupted me.

Jas, you are paying attention, Salayla said. That's rare for someone your age. I don't think the other new girls and *lighties* are paying attention. Too busy with their loud parties and their public drunkenness, which is very offensive in a Mozzy neighborhood, you know. Very offensive. *Ja,* things are changing in the Bo-Kaap. It may be permanent, and it may be for the worse. It's already permanent for my children. They can't afford to live here; they can't afford to live much of anywhere. That's because they can't find work, and to be honest with you, my dear, that's a greater concern to me than the end of our family legacy in the Bo-Kaap. For you must know that we do have a legacy here. Mine and my husband's family, we have been here for as long as anyone can remember. His family grew up in this very house on Chiappini Street, and when we had our children, we imagined that life would go on as usual. Possibly better than usual, because my husband and I scraped together the fees to send them to the colored universities that were designed to train the smarter colored people in a trade. Maybe it wasn't fancy literature or advanced mathematics, but it was the best at the time, and we thought they would have everything they needed to succeed in some sort of economy. Well. You must know that that economy is over. They can't even make money in other ways. My son became so desperate that he joined a street gang, thinking that a share of the *dagga* trade would be a steady paycheck. Of course we were barely able to get him out alive. I could have told him that dealing with *skollies* would be a disaster. *Ja,* that was hectic. And my poor daughter went and got married to a man who was no better than a *skollie* himself. No, my dear, we have no one to blame and everyone to blame for what has happened in this neighborhood and in this country. I stopped looking for answers a long time ago. Now I am just waiting for the day when we sell our home and move to Salt River, or maybe leave this whole bloody city. We will give the money from the house to our children and then try to support ourselves, as many of the older people in the Bo-Kaap are doing. Have you spoken to them, my dear? Have you noticed how many of them are in the same situation, with the old women doing dressmaking or taking in laundry, and the old men breaking themselves by hauling wood or digging ditches for some *poppy* in Camps Bay? Sheesh, man. We cannot continue like this for long. Soon we will all be scattered all over, so don't be surprised. For as long as I have known this country things have been this way, changing fast and permanently and possibly for the worst. Pay attention, my dear. There will be more to follow.

Salayla had interrupted the course of my speech. According to my programming, I was to pause after offering enlightenment on the cause of the troubles in the Bo-Kaap before proceeding with an explanation of my ideas for action. Those ideas—zoning controls, mandatory fair valuations for homes going on the market, mandatory payments into a community fund for every tour bus and video shoot—deflated with every word Salayla spoke. I turned and walked down the steps of her stoop with a weak farewell, and I plodded across the street with my head drooping between my shoulders.

Later that day Keith knocked on my door. I invited him in for tea and resumed pacing the kitchen floor. Occasionally I stole glances at him, furious searching glances, and I muttered and bit my nails. Keith crossed his legs and sipped his tea, smiling. At length he said, I see you have had your first encounter. If I may venture to ask—

Oh, stop it, I said. They're failing themselves and their children, and all because they refuse to believe us about the urgency of the situation. They have never lived through a gentrification process, and they cannot appreciate the fact that everything they have worked for is in direct and immediate peril.

Look, Keith said. I get angry, too. But the truth is that they have seen other colored neighborhoods within this city cleared out and razed to the ground. They are highly conscious of what it means to lose a community, and even if they have been so politically incapacitated by their determination to keep the Bo-Kaap intact throughout a century that was designed to destroy it you must never, never presume that you understand better than they do. They may choose not to put up a fight to save this neighborhood. If that is what they decide, there will be nothing either you or I can do, apart from gnashing our teeth and howling in agony. And if they come to that decision, it will not be because they do not understand what an annihilated community is like. Remember that. You have seen it, but they have lived it. Then he smiled into his teacup.

I tried to remember Keith's words without hating him as I went about my neighborhood rounds. With each conversation I grew more agitated. My neighbors offered ingenious excuses for why they were unable to organize around the gentrification question in their community, many of them having to do with the time demands of preoccupations such as sheep keeping, but all I heard was a lack of interest. They listened, but they were not moved, and when I think about it now, their resistance may have had something to do with the ever-increasing bitterness of the messenger. The other point that occurs to me now, with some amusement, is the fact that I avoided those homes where my fashionable new neighbors were living. They may have proven more receptive to my mission; they probably had the same fears and feelings of anger as I did.

So I decided to give my speech to someone in a position to take decisive action. I have no idea why I thought this would work. Keith warned me against it. He said that we should approach authority only when we had the measurable support of the neighborhood. Otherwise, he said, we will diminish the credibility of our complaint;

we may even cause harm to our cause. I brushed his words aside. I believed that having the support of the people—whatever that meant—would have been ideal, of course, but short of that, securing approval from someone who was in a position to make our vision real would suffice. What I also believed, though I was unable to admit it even to myself, was that I was not up to the task of inspiring my neighbors to take the actions that I considered in their best interest.

So one afternoon I walked over to the Ministry of Housing Affairs. It had been difficult to schedule the appointment. Many South African officials have little time to hear local concerns; to get an audience, I had to mention that I occasionally worked for an international news outlet. This indiscretion bothered me, and I walked into a functionary's office feeling suspicious about his attitude toward the public. That feeling swelled when he looked up from the paperwork in front of him and, instead of offering me a chair, said that he considered his decision to grant me an audience regarding a local civilian concern to be an exception in the personal protocols he had established for himself and his office. I thanked him for the exception and told him I was certain that what I had to share would not be a waste of his time. Then I walked toward his desk in the hope that he might invite me to sit down. Perhaps he would have made his invitation sooner had he not been busily probing his inner nostrils with all the fingers on the hand he would shortly extend to me, but he was, and I tried to disguise my horror with a placid smile. He was a sour-looking man with skin the color of a dried Calimyrna fig. In ten years he would resemble the men who wear nubbly white skullcaps and gather outside the

Bo-Kaap mosques in the evening with canes and leather-bound Korans, assuming, of course, that those men still gather there. In ten years those men may have relocated to parched suburbs like Bellville and Milnerton, and the mosques may be loft spaces. The short route to both of those possibilities began when the dignitary ceased mining his nose and grabbed hold of my hand.

Sit, he said, and say what you will. Just remember that we have deadlines and constraints in this country.

Sir, I've come to talk to you about an opportunity in the Bo-Kaap, I said. The people of that neighborhood should have the chance to profit from the use others make of their community, and I have an idea that will enhance government revenue if officials choose to partner with us in preserving the neighborhood as part of the country's national heritage. The Bo-Kaap itself is a resource, and all resources must cost the user something. Take, for example, a film company that is interested in shooting part of a video in the neighborhood. The government could levy a day-use fee, which might then go into a community fund to pay for streetlights or road repair in the area. Or, in the event of development, officials could negotiate with companies that are looking to build by asking them to create some low-income housing units along with their projects—

My God, the idle speculation, he snorted. Is this what you American journalists do all day? Let me slow you down before you go any further. Why should the Bo-Kaap receive streetlights and road repair when so many of the townships in Cape Town, like Khayelitsha or Nyanga, if you have left the Bo-Kaap long enough to know where black South Africans live, don't have running water or proper electricity? As for development, we are not in a position to demand much from anyone who wants to do safe development in South Africa. Especially if they want to develop in a poverty-stricken neighborhood of colored people.

Listen, my dear, he said. The battle has not finished in this country. Sheesh, man, it's only begun. Take, for example, your Bo-Kaap. I don't believe anyone from that neighborhood has set foot inside a South African government office for at least a century. No problem or cause was big enough for them to issue a complaint, not even the transformation of this country. Therefore the Bo-Kaap owes as much to us as we owe to them, and we tend to take a wide view of the concept of community. So, my dear. You must understand the situation in South Africa. Under the last government the Bo-Kaap earned its special privileges by providing the city of Cape Town with a cheap and cheerful labor force. If you are wondering what I mean by special privileges, try running water. Try garbage collection. Try the electrical grid. Sheesh, man, try the fact that the Bo-Kaap still exists. There are a lot of colored areas that weren't so lucky, to say nothing of the black areas.

That doesn't mean the Bo-Kaap doesn't have problems, I began.

But he started waving that hand again, and he said, *Ja, ja*, of course, there is poverty and unemployment; there is crime and there are gangs. Listen, my dear, I don't mean to say those problems are small. They are nothing to trifle with. But most colored neighborhoods share those problems, and I must assure you that nearly all the black neighborhoods are suffering the same. So while I agree with you most wholeheartedly that it is time for us to look at ways to partner with developers seeking to build in the Bo-Kaap, I would challenge you to agree that it is time for the Bo-Kaap to make a contribution to the renewal of this country. And it may be that in making that contribution, the Bo-Kaap comes to look different from the neighborhood you feel sentimental about. It may be a worthwhile change if it gives other areas in this country the opportunity to feel what it's like to live in a genuine community.

When I walked outside I saw Keith leaning against the wall, smoking a cigarette. I had told him that I would be going to the ministry against his advice; he had listened impassively. His only question had been the time of my appointment. As I walked over to meet him I felt, in a cold and sudden tremor, the poignancy of his response and the fullness of his life, and when I fell, weeping, into his arms, it was not for myself or even for the residents of the Bo-Kaap that I was crying. I would have buried both my shame and his in his arms if I could have done so. I could not, and he knew it. We didn't speak for a long time. And as we walked side by side through the National Gardens, which once provided shade for the select number of people who were permitted to live in the city center but now sheltered ragged tramps of all colors, I was unsure whether we would speak for a long time to come. But as we passed the National Library Keith lit another cigarette and looked at my devastated face for a moment. Then he began to speak slowly and with a softness I had not heard in his voice before and have not heard since.

So I will guess that my good friends in the ministry did not offer you what you were seeking, he said. If I know them well enough, they claimed that they had more pressing obligations to which they must tend—obligations in places that matter, perhaps, places that were supportive during the critical moments of their ascension. Perhaps they exhibited some perverse pleasure upon learning about the trouble in the Bo-Kaap. Many of those in that particular ministry grew up in colored townships like the one I grew up in, a township that was far-flung and dusty and mean; and when they think of the Bo-Kaap, they think of pressing their noses to the glass of a beautiful store. Forgive them for their pettiness. Take pride in your courage, whatever the outcome may be. I did not advise you to do this, but I do admire you for trying to take this matter straight to the top. Only by doing so could you have learned for yourself that this is most certainly an instance where those who lead do not have the approval of the whole flock. That has never been a unique problem in this country, but I have the feeling it will come as a shock to the people of the Bo-Kaap and that it will remain a problem under what we now call democracy. It will come as a shock to them because they do not yet understand how democracy works. Perhaps you considered this as you went from house to house and continued to fail at your mission of motivating someone, anyone, to present our troubles as a community to the government. If you did not consider it then, consider it now. It was not simply your lack of skill at persuasion, and that was why I sent you to do it. I wanted you to see for yourself the work we must do here first. We cannot hope to save the spirit of this neighborhood if no one here recognizes what we must do to save it. That is a lesson that only democracy can teach, and we are unused to democracy here. I am afraid that this community may be obliterated under the pressure of more expedient concerns before there is an apprehension of how democracy rewards those who are passionate and undivided and punishes those who are passionate and alone. I presume from the expression on your face that by bringing this matter to the attention of our friends in the ministry that you may have helped to destroy all that you love here. But you may also have expedited the democratic learning process; you may have given the people here the opportunity to choose what it is they wish for as a community and what they must do to make that choice their reality. I would have wished for this community to come to that conclusion by themselves rather than at the behest of an outsider. But now that it is done, content yourself with the positive impact that your involvement may have. Sometimes it takes the intervention of someone from the outside to show us the pain and deprivation that is alive within our midst.

We turned onto Wale Street as Keith finished speaking. Wale Street is one of Cape Town's main downtown arteries; at the busy intersection of Buitengracht Street it slices into the pastel world of the Bo-Kaap and morphs into Upper Wale Street. No words passed between us as we hiked the several blocks to Buitengracht. As we stood on the corner and waited for the traffic light to change, I gazed into the snow globe of my neighborhood and marveled at the new tears on my cheeks. Keith looked at them, too, and as we stood on the traffic island and felt our sides shiver from the speed of passing cars, we saw each other around the tears that had been waiting patiently to flow from both of us. Somehow in making themselves visible the tears ceased to exert their hold on us. We smiled at each other. There was hurt and there was grief in those smiles.

While I was saving the Bo-Kaap, my grandmother Joyce I was dying in Louisiana.

She was eighty-three years old, but no one had expected her to die. She had survived three heart attacks and twenty years with diabetes and annual bouts of pneumonia, so when she went to the hospital with a bronchial infection she declared herself in fine health. And so she was. But they kept her at the hospital, and that is when the facts surrounding her case begin to turn cloudy. As for the ones that remain clear, I suspect they are linked, though how I do not know: the first fact is that Joyce I was concerned about her eldest son, John, and his second wife, Dolores. She did not trust them, and she was worried about the way they were treating her youngest son, Louis. The second fact is that when my mother called from California for news of Joyce I's condition, she found it difficult to get any information. The doctors were reticent, ill-informed, or haphazard in their conversations, and my mother suspected that they were treating Joyce I with the cheerful neglect that many health professionals in this country offer to those who are old and poor. The family members who were gathering around Joyce I's bedside— including John and Dolores; Joyce I's eldest sister, Shirley; and Louis and his girlfriend Cassandra—did not report the news in a way that made my mother feel comforted. Somehow the telephone was always passed to Dolores, who discouraged my mother from coming without offering any concrete evidence in one or another direction. After several days passed and Joyce I remained in the hospital, my mother made an intuitive decision and flew to Louisiana anyway. By the time she arrived, Joyce I had lost consciousness.

My mother relieved the others from their vigil and spent the last twenty-six hours of her mother's life in the chair beside her. She read to her from the book of John, committing the fourteenth chapter, which was Joyce I's favorite, to memory. She sang all the songs she remembered Joyce I singing to her at bedtime and all the songs she remembered Joyce I singing in the fields; and when she had exhausted her knowledge of those songs, she held Joyce I's hand and sang her the songs she used to sing to me. That is what she was doing, twenty-six hours into her vigil, when Joyce I breathed for the last time.

At this point it was my mother's wish to plan a burial and pursue an investigation into the cause of Joyce I's death, a question that remains unanswered to this day. Unfortunately my mother was not aware of the enmity in which some of her siblings held her until it reached catastrophic proportions. Now, when she considers her position, my mother berates herself for thinking that placing herself at a geographic, cultural, and socioeconomic remove would be enough to spare her from the gnashing resentments of her family. She had seen it in the behavior of her brothers. John and Louis are incorrigible alcoholics, and they feuded constantly until Louis left Louisiana a few months before Joyce I's death. My mother declined to comment on the fighting and did what she could to assist them— sending money for Louis's son, for instance, and buying a home in Palmetto for John and Dolores to rent from her when they could not find a place to live. She invited Shane, her sister Sandra's child, to live with our family for a summer; she would have kept him longer, I believe, had my father not objected. She bought Christmas presents and paid for broken transmissions, and through these gestures, perhaps, she imagined she might spare herself from the anger of which only her elder sister Berneice had been willing to speak:

It took me a long time with you, Berneice said. With the hate.

They were sitting on their mother's porch about ten years before her death. The day had been hot, and in the distance my mother could see the brick-red earth of Palmetto steaming. It was early evening; the sky looked like the crushed-velvet lining of a jewelry box. Soon, my mother thought. As soon as night fell and the crickets' sound rose to a cacophony, the earth would begin to smoke. When that happened she would have to go inside, because the smoke would whip up into a creamlike consistency and she would no longer be able to see in front of her. She did not like that. People who walked up to the house out of that fog emerged too suddenly, and everything about them looked sunken. Both ghost and person, she thought and then she turned to Berneice.

What are you talking about? she said.

It took me a long time to get over hating you, Berneice said. I hated you for a long time. Hated Mother for longer, if it makes you feel better. But I don't hate either of you anymore.

Why? my mother said.

Because you got to go, Berneice said. She got you out, and I thought it should have been me. I was older than you. Why shouldn't it have been me? What was wrong with me? You're never going to know how many mornings I asked myself those questions. I'd be stumbling out of our house after Daddy had finally passed out from drinking. He'd be getting his sleep, and the way I saw it he had taken that sleep from me. Because he couldn't sleep unless he'd been fucking with us all night. Chasing us out of the house. Shooting at us. Smacking those boys around. Felt like he needed to do that to get to bed. So I'd run through the cornfield trying to get away from him, but I still had to get to school on time or pick the greens before the sun scorched the curls off the nape of my neck. That was what I had to do while you were lounging under the palm trees. Least that's what I thought you were doing. And I thought it should have been me because I was a tougher kid than you, and I thought I would have gone after California with everything I had and really made something of myself. Gotten us all out of here. That was part of the reason I ran away from home in the first place—I wanted to prove I could really make something of myself. Well.

She paused here and my mother took advantage of the moment to consider whether Berneice was drunk. She remembered that Berneice had not had anything to drink that day—their sister had been supervising the alcohol, and she and Berneice were very close. Berneice did her best to behave for Sandra. And even if she had been drinking, Berneice's weakness for alcohol had never been an impairment to her honesty.

So I got over hating you, Berneice said. I just wanted you to know that. Took some doing. But it took a lot less for me to get over you than it took for me to get over Mother.

Silence fell and the crickets rushed to fill it. My mother stared straight out from the porch into the steaming fields beyond. Berneice lit a cigarette and stared out with her. Hmm, she said after a few moments. What do you think, Joyce? Think I can get Sandra to loosen her grip on my stash?

From Joyce II's perspective, her opportunity to leave for California was also her opportunity to grow up without her mother. No opportunity California gave her could have been commensurate with that loss. Many of her decisions make sense only in light of this. When she was modeling, for example, she may have found herself on the pages of *GQ* magazine, but she didn't see any of the money. She sent it all back to Louisiana so that Joyce I could have indoor bathrooms in her home in Palmetto. She may have gone to Rome and Paris, but she went without food when she returned to San Jose State. What was the point of eating when I was paid to stay skinny? my mother said when I asked her about it. Now I think she was brave for making light of the situation, but I wish she had been in Palmetto to see her siblings' faces on the day the contractor appeared. She was not there, could not have been there—she was working to pay for him to be there in her stead—and so she had to pay for those bathrooms in the late 1960s and she had to pay for them when she came to bury her mother in the spring of 2002.

After Joyce I's passing, my mother assumed responsibility for her funeral and her legal arrangements. She had asked all five of her siblings if any of them would be willing to take responsibility for the planning and the financing of what was to become an extraordinarily expensive set of events. Four of her siblings demurred on account of poverty and one demurred on account of delicacy and helplessness. So my mother said that she would divide the cost of the funeral six ways and accept their contributions as they were able to repay her. As she set out to make the preparations it became gradually clear to her that the reason why some of her siblings had refused to assist with burial arrangements was that they were preoccupied with plans of their own.

My mother got her first inkling of those alternative arrangements on the night before she had scheduled a family viewing of Joyce I's body at a local funeral home. Shirley's eldest children, Mirna and Virby—two of the children my mother had helped her to raise—had flown in from Southern California that afternoon. Shirley, Mirna, Virby, and my mother made plans to spend the next several nights at Joyce I's house, as John and Dolores could not house four guests at the home they were renting from my mother. (They had opened their home to Shirley and my mother while Joyce I was in the hospital.) At some unknown point, Shirley changed her mind about leaving John and Dolores. My mother remained unaware of this reversal until late in the evening, as she stood outside John's house with her suitcase and a small grocery bag of food she had purchased for the next morning's breakfast. John pulled up in his van, and my mother loaded her suitcase inside while he watched from the driver's seat. A few minutes passed. Impatient, he blew his horn and shouted for Shirley. After a few moments of his honking and hollering—my mother tried not to laugh—Shirley and Dolores walked out to the porch in no particular hurry. Dolores settled into an old rocking chair while Shirley descended the steps to talk with my mother, who was inquiring as to the whereabouts of Shirley's luggage. Shirley explained that she had changed her mind and would be declining the invitation to stay with her children and her sister; then, without a pause, she demanded to know what my mother was carrying in the grocery bag.

My mother opened the bag. Milk, she said. And cereal. But Shirley, why—

That's my milk, Shirley said. And with a vindictive expression as if to remind my mother that our most vicious acts are always our solutions to the most quotidian concerns, she snatched the milk carton out of my mother's hands with enough force to send her stumbling backward.

Though shocked, my mother had the presence of mind to shout that it was her milk, not Shirley's. I bought it an hour ago, my mother said. I bought it for tomorrow—

You took my milk, Shirley said, shaking the carton at my mother, and it was then that Dolores said from her perch on the porch that my mother had no right to take other people's belongings.

But I guess I can't be surprised, Dolores said with a sniff. Everyone knows you think you're so special. Can't expect you to be considerate of other folks.

My mother stood there stunned as John, who had watched the drama unfold without a word, climbed out of his van and took her by the elbow. She twisted her head to stare soundlessly while he escorted her into the van and closed the passenger door. He inched down the unpaved driveway and into the main road while my mother continued to gawk at the women's cold mean faces. Standing out of the thick gray fog and trapped in the molding of John's headlights, my mother thought, their features were frozen in bas-relief. This made her wonder whether the venom to which she had just been exposed was the result of their personalities or the remnant of some ancient curse. She had ample opportunity to ponder this question over the next several days, although this first incident was so bizarre in its origins, and so frightening in its implications, that my mother would have been willing to ignore it. Unfortunately it was followed by further incidents that she could not ignore—the silence with which all of her siblings greeted her when she marched into the funeral home the following morning, for instance. Nor could she ignore the fact that she was late for the viewing because John had failed to drive her, Mirna, and Virby as he had promised and she had had to borrow a car and hunt for the funeral home by herself. She was finding it more and more difficult to quell her own apprehension, much less that of her niece and nephew. (What is going on? Mirna kept asking, in a whisper, and with the same fearful countenance my mother recognized from when she used to tell her ghost stories when they were little.) And she certainly could not ignore her brother when he stormed into Joyce I's house on the afternoon of the viewing and said that he was going to kill her.

He had been drinking, but since John was usually drinking my mother found it difficult to press that fact into service as an extenuating circumstance. His movements were loose and erratic as he crashed into Joyce I's house. He spun about with a lamp in the living room, foot caught in the cord, and released a string of curses—curses that were redirected at my mother when he stumbled into Joyce I's bedroom. Among the accusations he launched at her, all of which were confirmed by others who had come into contact with John and Dolores during this time, were charges of selfishness and conceit. Perhaps the most hurtful charge was that my mother waltzed down to Louisiana once a year to take Joyce I to "the big house," where she bought her dinners of shrimp cocktail before jetting back to California, leaving Joyce I's daily care in the hands of more loyal children, such as John and Dolores. After completing this torrent of abuse, John told my mother that he was going to kill her. He said this twice. Mirna and Virby were standing in the kitchen as he shouted. My mother was sitting on Joyce I's brass-framed bed. The brass had worn off all the bedposts to reveal a worn shade of gray. Sitting across from my mother on an old patchwork-upholstered footstool was a representative from the insurance agency with which Joyce I had done business. My mother had called the agency to discover whether or not Joyce I had taken out any policies that might defray the cost of her funeral. Rita Fontenot, the insurance representative, was telling my mother that Joyce I had not.

Rita Fontenot was possessed of tremendous powers, my mother said. In my mother's time she may have been the type of woman who would have drawn all the neighborhood women to her back door under cover of dusk. The women would come clutching their luck charms and the scraps of paper onto which they had scribbled the name of the man they desired or the relative in trouble, and they would cross themselves and glance about with growing fear as one by one they passed through her door. My mother called these women the numbers women. Other people may have called them something else, but that's what my mother called them. And what she said was that they needed to acquire not just the power to effect magic but also the capacity to take their customers' troubles deep into the recesses of their own hearts. They had to look deep into the places where they saw each and every one of their own fears and pains stripped to its root. Only when they recognized the full source of their customers' pain—which was in fact the full source of their own pain—could the numbers women help. My mother believed it was this emotional capacity that made the numbers women so few and far between. She would say that there were plenty of hoodoo women out there, but they were useless because magic was the easy part. Most of us who have been here for long enough have something in the blood, she told me. Most of us who come from the families in these parts have it in us to cast a spell or have a dream or get a curse going. But we can't make them work, or we can't make them work right, and that's because we're not feeling each other for what to do. We're not hearing what the real problem is. She said you had to open up every part of your body and take in the full register of what you were hearing—not just the words but the timbre of the voice and the depth of the tonalities and the feelings that come out, not what they say they feel but what you can hear from everything else. And most of the time they don't even recognize those feelings themselves. They can't even get that their problem is based on some personal emotion that doesn't have anything to do with the matter at hand. That's why they can't deal with the problem, because they've blocked themselves off from what's really going on, and that's the reason most of these women out here, running around calling themselves hoodoo women, can't do nothing for nobody. That's what my mother would tell me, and she said that if I ever found a numbers woman I should fall to my knees and give thanks to the Lord. For not only had I found a woman who had the power to cure what ailed me, but I had found a woman who could show me how to break through whatever I had put up against my own pain. Well. I would have liked for my mother to have met Rita Fontenot. Rita Fontenot did not do the numbers, but she knew what to do when she recognized my pain. When John left the house after making his grand pronouncement, she turned to look at me and saw that I could not even cry. She said nothing to me about that, choosing to call for Mirna and Virby instead. Together the four of us made several decisions. The first was that we (me in particular) needed our own transportation. Don't you depend on him, Rita Fontenot told us, and in fact the second decision we made was that Virby would return the car John had left at Joyce I's house days ago, presumably for our use. Virby left to do this, and Rita Fontenot rose to her feet and made that afternoon's final decision on her own: She would interrupt her plans for the rest of the afternoon and drive us to the car rental desks at the airport. Before I could shake off the stupor of my shock to protest against this remarkable show of generosity, we were loaded into her car and off to Opelousas. It was a journey of half an hour and Mirna held my hand the entire way. I remember Rita Fontenot tuning her radio to hear about the traffic on the highways we would be taking, and I remember her lowering the volume on the radio to tell me that I should feel free to weep as much as I needed to in her car. Nothing's going to happen to you in here, she said, and I marveled that she knew exactly what I needed but could not do. Instead I gazed out the window at the dome of the blue sky and the good red earth and the straight gray ridge of highway that ran straight into them as if it could take us into some unknown original space between them and I wondered when the fog would

come. Then we got to Opelousas and there were no cars. It was
Easter weekend, they all said. Maybe you should try at Lafayette.
Lafayette was thirty-five miles in the other direction, and by now
the sky was turning to ink, but Rita Fontenot opened her car doors
and started her engine. We climbed in and resumed our previous
occupations—Mirna with my hand, Rita with her radio—and halfway
through that drive I began to cry. It was turning dark outside and
dark in the car, and Mirna and Rita Fontenot sat in silence as I
bowed my head and quivered with sobs. And as it all came out it occurred to me that I had never felt so relieved as I did in the presence
of those two women that night. And I believe that they felt something during that drive to Lafayette as well, some easing of their
own pain and fear as they listened to me sob, because when we got
to the airport and discovered they had no cars either we were all
calm. We just stood inside the rental office and waited, and when a
representative from one of the agencies ran in at ten o'clock that
night to tell us that someone had returned a car against all expectations, we regarded him with the cool unsurprise of a group who
knew that the car had been ours all along. There lay ahead of us the
matter of how to return to Palmetto in the dark, but about even that
we were unconcerned. I will admit feeling a tremor of fear when I
climbed behind the wheel of that rental car and saw that the fog had
drawn its full strength from the sun above it and the earth beneath it
and I would be driving into a cold white sea. I like to believe that I
would have been able to drive us back to Palmetto on my own. I like
to believe that I would have found the way even though I lose my
bearings while driving to the corner grocery store, but that was not

a point I had to prove that night. Rita Fontenot, whose graciousness was beginning to lift her above the fog in my eyes, offered to lead us back to Palmetto before returning to her own home in the Lafayette area. Mirna and I climbed into our rental car and floated along behind the snowy glow of Rita Fontenot's taillights like lost gold miners following the sunlight at the end of a shaft. I can't imagine a trustier guide or a safer journey.

My mother's return to Palmetto brought about a shift in her fortunes. She and Mirna walked into Joyce I's house to find her brother Louis and his girlfriend Cassandra waiting for them. Louis and Cassandra had begun to formulate doubts about the accusations they had heard from John and Dolores. They keep saying you want to be in charge of everything, Louis said. You're the one shitting in high cotton, so you think you can be the boss. But you asked if anyone would help you—I know you asked that. The four of them sat down to discuss what they knew, and slowly my mother began to understand the nature of the enemy she was facing. (That understanding crystallized for her during her mother's funeral, when Dolores twice interrupted the proceedings to ask my mother if she could have Joyce I's Bible and the floral arrangement on which it stood. In both instances my mother refused her request. Somehow the Bible and the arrangement came into Dolores's possession anyway.) Over the next few days, while she finished organizing Joyce I's burial and tombstone, my mother sought out as much information as she could find about the situation in Palmetto. She discovered that she had been inattentive for too long. Dolores boasted manipulative skills my mother could not hope to match, and she had experienced great success fanning the resentments of my mother's relatives. (But *why?* my mother said. Cassandra said that the only person who could answer that for certain was Dolores, but that she had noticed that Dolores removed all of Joyce I's food from her house as soon as Joyce I went into the hospital. And that move, Cassandra said, marks her in my book as a grade-A bitch with more nerve than a brass-assed monkey.) One person Dolores had not been able to turn was Berneice, and though Sandra lived nearby she had her doubts as well. But for the most part, as my mother uncovered wellsprings of hatred among her cousins and uncles and neighbors, she chose to confide in no one. Instead she stayed in Joyce I's house and occupied herself with the innumerable tasks left undone: distributing the most prized of Joyce I's possessions among her siblings, packing the less prized possessions into boxes, arranging for storage containers, hiring moving men. She asked Cassandra to stay with her after Mirna left for California. She and Cassandra were in the last stages of removing all evidence of Joyce I from her home when my father arrived.

We failed my mother. All of us.

When Joyce I died, when she was buried, when her daughter was enduring assaults of all kinds, my father and my brother and I were absent. We have our excuses, of course. My brother was taking his second-year examinations at Stanford Law School. My father was escorting several of his undergraduate students on a research trip to Detroit. I was living abroad. These are our excuses. They matter only inasmuch as they were what we had to cling to after leaving my mother in the hands of strangers and enemies during the time she needed us most. My father did appear in Louisiana eventually and for three days he did help with the final arrangements for Joyce I's departure from this world. He was not able to contact John and Dolores during his visit, and the full weight of his deficiency must have collapsed atop him as soon as they flew back to California. My mother opened the door to their bedroom and placed her suitcase on the floor and her face exploded in a current of tears that she found impossible to stop. She took to her bed. When I called during this time I spoke mostly to my father, and neither of us had much to say. A heavy burden of helplessness squatted dumbly between us as I stammered silly questions and my father spoke of how my mother, freed from physical threat, had finally allowed herself to grieve for the mother to whom she had never been close enough.

I was thinking of my grandmother and my mother when I went to a town in South Africa called Orania. I was thinking of these two women and these two women only—not my small-minded aunts and uncles, not my uncle's dog-hearted wife, not the whole reprehensible cast of cousins and relations who had swarmed around my mother and her adversary, eager to snap off an ankle here or a knuckle joint there—because for me, the family ties were inconsequential. My grandmother denied my mother her presence during many of the important moments in my mother's life. I denied my mother my presence during the last important moment in my grandmother's life. And after I heard the stories of the funeral I drew the conclusion that no more family links remained to be broken. Had I not gone to Orania, I may have lost faith even in what does remain for me and these two women: a heavy brass-framed bed covered with handmade quilts, a spine-cracked Bible, a quiet hour to spend with pictures of California, and our dreams. All of our dreams.

I hadn't wanted to go to Orania. Like most people I found the concept of Orania offensive: a town limited to settlement by Afrikaners. I considered it irrelevant, a throwback, and I certainly didn't imagine that there would be anything for me to learn there, because then they would have needed to know something to teach me. Perhaps as a result of my grumbling attitude, Tom Masland took glee in making the suggestion.

Go with Per, Tom said. He's made some contacts up there.

Per was an exceptional photographer. He was also Swedish, and I had the feeling that his experience in Orania would be quite a bit different from mine. I must have looked less than enthusiastic, because Tom pressed: Look, you mustn't be afraid to cover anyone. Especially people you don't agree with. Now just go up there and see what kind of community they're scratching out of the desert. It'll be a good opportunity for you to spend some time in a small town.

Can't you send me to cover a civil war or something? I said. You know I don't like small towns—

Tom began chuckling. Yeah, yeah, he said. It'll be cool. Besides, they're pretty interesting. They get along with the new government; they get along with their neighbors. They say they don't need anything from anybody. Just like someone else I know.

I started to protest again but Tom had already turned away from me. He was digging around on his desk for a phone number. Call Per, he said. And get in touch with this guy, the town spokesman. I spoke to him a few days ago. He was quoting Robert Owen like a street preacher with the book of Hebrews. People say the whole town's nuts like that. It'll be good for you to spend a couple of days up there.

I did call Per, and a few weeks later I met John Strydom, the man with whom Tom had had the pleasure of speaking. Per and I made a six-hour drive into the dust and sand of the Northern Cape province. When we arrived, in a black Mercedes crusted with dirt, Strydom met us at the town's general store. He drove an old Volkswagen hatchback. He was a tall, thin man with wire-rimmed eyeglasses and a slivered mustache. That day he wore a light blue short-sleeved button-down shirt in a cheap crepey fabric and well-pressed khakis with a dull shine to them. Everything about him suggested prideful restraint in the face of privation. He was not a man who wasted anything, even gestures. As we approached he watched us without so much as an extra blink to expose his thoughts. Then he offered brisk handshakes and opened the passenger door of his car. Come, he said to me. Your photographer knows the town; he can go on his own. But I think you should come with me.

I imagine that you want to know how we are building this and how we are making a living out of the desert, was the first thing he said after we buckled our seat belts and drove away. Per was waving at us from his perch next to the Mercedes. With a stab of fear, I watched him shrink, still waving, into the dust that surrounded us. When he was gone, I directed my attention to John Strydom, who was pointing out some of the small, neat cinder-block homes that new residents had built. You might notice how we don't have good and bad parts of town here, he said. Everyone who lives here is expected to have pride of ownership in what we have. *Jas,* we worked hard to get it.

The original Orania was a rudimentary village for employees of the Department of Water Affairs and Forestry while they built a canal system beneath the nearby Vanderkloof Dam in the 1960s. As the desert climate of this area is forbidding, with roasting days and cold-snap nights, the employees found it to their advantage to make their temporary home as comfortable as possible. They cleared wide main roads and built a basic network for electricity distribution. The workers had also built many of the older wooden clapboard houses, and as far as I could tell these homes continued to carry out their original purpose of housing large groups of restless young men. I didn't remember to ask John Strydom if the government workers had also built the town's water purification plant, which made it possible for Oranians to drink from the Orange River. I am still angry at myself for neglecting that question, for it would have been nice to know if the South African government made Orania's further development possible with the construction of that plant. The Orange River is the only source of water in the area, and it is not fit for direct consumption. The cost of importing purified water or setting up distribution from a distant water source might have prohibited Orania from further growth. Now, as I write this, the dependence of Orania's utopia on the Orange River and the goodwill of the national government strikes me as its potential fatal flaw.

John Strydom drove me tirelessly around the property—Orania is in fact not an incorporated town but a substantial piece of private land developed and managed by Orania Management Services (Pty.)

Ltd. and administered and managed by Vluytjeskraal Share-block Limited—and showed me all that the Oranians had built to sustain themselves. He showed me the airport (two airstrips, the first 1,300 meters and the second 1,000 meters). He pointed out the community center with swimming pool and tennis courts. He mentioned that there were canoes available to rent from a local entrepreneur who had also developed a caravan park on the banks of the Orange River. We drove by some of the other industries that the residents had developed—a doctor's office, a hairdresser's, a café, a hardware store, a mechanic's garage—and Strydom waved hello to every person he saw. All of them waved in reply. He explained to me how the residents got their mail and their money. ABSA Bank, a national enterprise, maintained an office that was staffed once a week; the town council office maintained a postal agency with limited hours. Then Strydom drove me to the development of which he was most proud: a 2,000-hectare farm. The town purchased the farm a year after its founding, Strydom said, and since we've irrigated it, we've produced some of the most beautiful fruits you've ever seen. Won't you step out and have a look?

With caution I opened the car door and stepped out. We stood in the shade of pecan trees—more than twenty thousand of them, I later found out. All about I heard the hiss of insects, the gentle flaying of sprinklers, the crinkle of leaves. Strydom reached up and plucked a fresh green nut from a tree. He rolled it in his palm as he spoke; his voice, which had been clipped and dry, grew soft and warm. Orania was founded on a principle of sustainable development, he said. Most outsiders think we are all about the sustainability of our culture, but we are just as interested in what it takes to live on this earth with respect for what we take and what we give. This farm, you must know, is an example. When the first residents moved here it was all a bit of a muddle. Bunch of bloody *okes* who didn't know about planting and doing their own work. Fortunately we all understand how important it is to be sparing with the resources we have been given; we know that God is under no obligation to give us any more. And we are a resourceful people. Look at what we have already made bloom in the desert. We are already exporting our melons, and soon we will export our pecans. We believe there is no better occupation for man than simple peaceful work to nourish the soil and the soul, so we are learning, quite literally, how to sustain ourselves. Those who knew how to plant and irrigate taught the *lighties* who didn't know. And our philosophy, so far at least, has worked. A few people who knew something about cows asked if anyone might be interested in starting a dairy, and the response was overwhelming. Now we've got a dairy with the most luscious creamy milk—no preservatives, none of that *kak*. Our goal is to be as self-sustainable as possible. Did you get that, miss? Please. It's important. For too long we believed what other people told us about what we needed to do in order to survive. All we need is the resources of our own minds and those that can be nurtured from the earth. And to be left alone from those who would tell us otherwise.

Should John Strydom ever have the opportunity to read this, I would like to assure him with the utmost sincerity that I did indeed get all of it. Orania was bought in 1991 by Professor Carel

Boshoff III. Boshoff III worked with a dozen like-minded friends to raise the necessary capital of 1.5 million rand from supporters around the country. The fact that he was able to raise money and organize a major land purchase from the apartheid government in 1991—the chaotic year during which that same government fell to shambles and the entire country stood poised on the brink of major civil conflict—speaks to the persistence of the Afrikaner dream of a *volkstaat*. In the last decade that dream has been pursued both in peace, as in Orania, and in bloodshed, by right-wing terrorist groups. Boshoff III told me that he had been dreaming of a *volkstaat* for thirty years. When I met him in his modest home in Orania, he poured me a cup of tea and told me that he considered Orania simply an experiment to show other Afrikaners how they too could win their freedom back after years of black rule. Some of us always knew it wasn't possible to maintain the so-called white land, the white country, he said. So we began a conversation to convince our people that we needed to prepare for the inevitable approach of black rule. Orania grew naturally out of that conversation, he said. He paused for a moment, then added, mostly to himself, that he had suffered dreadful disappointment when only a few hundred Afrikaners showed up to create his dream. I expected an initial turnout of thousands, he said with a sigh. And now, more than ten years on, we've still got only six hundred. I suppose Afrikaners have quite a bit invested in the republic, and a lot of fear, I'm sure, about losing their trinkets and their black labor. A lot of fear about doing their own work. But we'll see, miss, we'll see. The more the transformation of South Africa takes place, the more Afrikaners will

realize they are nothing but second-class citizens in this new dispen-
sation. And then Orania will see some growth, *jas*, of that you may
be sure. Of that you may be very sure.

I would have liked to hear more from Boshoff III about the
logistics of planning Orania, and I would definitely have liked to
have asked him a few questions about growing up with his grandfather, the apartheid prime minister H. F. Verwoerd. But John Strydom, who was once a journalist himself, sensed that Boshoff III
might not be the most media-friendly Orania representative. As my
host, driver, and escort (You must have an escort, you must have in-
troductions, he said to me) Strydom arranged my meetings and hov-
ered over many of my interviews. He felt this one rising to full
steam and broke in. Professor, he said, I think she should meet
your son. Boshoff III nodded gravely. Of course, he said. He's
in better touch with these young Afrikaners than I am. I'm an old
man, miss, an old man with old dreams and old pieces of the
past. I know I must be boring you. But you are welcome here. And
humor me—ask Mr. Strydom to take you to the Orania Museum.
There you'll see the detritus of my family. I'll soon belong to that
detritus myself. He smiled and motioned for John Strydom to help
him to his feet. He shuffled behind us to the door of his home. As
we drove off he lifted one hand in salute, keeping it raised long after
we had waved good-bye in return, like a lost voyager signaling a
passing ship.

Unfortunately, when Strydom placed a call to Carel Boshoff IV,
he learned that we couldn't meet that day. He scheduled a time for
the following afternoon and drove me to meet Per. I'll leave you for

now, he said. Per knows the town, and this evening he can introduce you to some of the friends he has made. Stay with him, and let me know if I can be of any assistance. He gave my hand a quick, dry shake before he drove off.

The guesthouse was full, so Strydom had made arrangements for us to sleep on cots in a shuttered clinic. (Orania was in the process of building a new, modern hospital.) It was cold in the clinic, and bats were nesting all over the building, and the corridors smelled of ammonia and death. Per and I didn't even negotiate about the amount of time we needed to spend there. As soon as we moved our luggage inside and examined our surroundings, we met in the hallway and exchanged two simple words: So. Interviews?

Our first interview, if that is what it may be called, was the only incident of real ugliness that weekend. Per and I went to a convenience store on the outskirts of town. As we walked out into the swirling dust, carrying our packets of dried fruit and bottled water, Per spotted an Oranian he had met. The man was a farmer in his early forties with a tall strapping build and a broad-brimmed hat. At his feet was an eager young dog, a Labrador retriever, which galloped toward us as soon as we came into view. I like dogs and crouched immediately to play with this one. That is what I was doing, several feet away, as Per said hello to his acquaintance and tried to strike up a conversation. The farmer said a few things to Per and then frowned at my back with enough force to snap me up and to attention. I turned to look at him. He strode toward me and grabbed his dog's collar, spitting in the direction of my ankle as he did so. Then he led the dog away. As he passed Per he nodded at him.

I will always remember the wheat-colored light that shaped the curve of the farmer's hat as he bent to seize his dog's collar, and the earthy singed smell of the dirt the dog kicked up as his owner led him away from me, but I hope for his own sake that Per can remember it far better than I. I fell very quiet after my confrontation with that farmer's failure of imagination; Per, on the other hand, could not stop talking. He insisted that few other Oranians would behave that way; he took me to meet a number of others—hairdressers, field hands, a young couple being wed that weekend—who proved their courtesy. They all told me that I was welcome, and they all gave the same answers when I asked what had brought them to Orania. The crime in mainstream South Africa was always the first answer, and the second, more studied answer had to do with pride in Afrikaner culture.

It's nice to be here with my family and speak our language and do things as we're used to doing them, said one hairdresser. Asked to expand on which sorts of things they were used to doing, she paused and then said, with wonder, Why—I guess I mean all of it, the *boerwurst braais* and the rides in the back of the *bakkie* and celebrating the Day of the Vow. The things I did as a child.

It's not easy to be a white man under the new government, said a field hand who lived in one of the rickety original barracks. I couldn't get any work. So I said to myself, *jassus*, this *kak* has to end. I've got to go somewhere where people appreciate what I can do, a place where it's not so bad to be Afrikaans.

I want my children to learn Afrikaans, said the young bride-to-be. And you know, in the schools outside of here, they don't teach it. It's something bad.

On the whole, I noticed a lack of self-reflection on the part of the Oranians, a certain fear of any internal debate that might lead to discomfort. When I asked to attend the wedding that would be taking place that weekend—Per would be there, taking photos— I was interrupted with a lavish flood of cheerful, incoherent excuses. When the wedding was over Per came to me with a simple explanation: Colored people were forbidden to enter the church. They didn't tell you? he said with a slight smile that faded quickly. They told me a long time ago.

Because of all the things that I knew I was not being told, the next day I approached Carel Boshoff IV's house with trepidation. The professor met me at the door. With a nod and that odd phrase— "You are welcome here"—he invited me in. I took off my shoes and made my way toward the living room. His eyes bore into my back all the way down the hall.

Boshoff IV was a provincial parliamentary representative for the Freedom Front party and an intellectual; I do not think it irrelevant to note that his home was unkempt. He had a lean, jaundiced body and a sharp wedge of nose. His bottom teeth were small and prominent. He folded himself into a chair in the living room and invited me to sit next to him. As we drank tea from chipped cups and dirty saucers he explained his opinion of how Orania was founded on a principle that was inclusive rather than exclusive. Our community is open to anyone who shares our mission, he said. Our mission is to live in favor of the Afrikaner identity—the Afrikaner ethnicity, culture, and political system. You have seen a bit of what that means: attention to the needs of our fellow men and attention to the land on which we live. So we refuse to use other kinds of people to do our work; in fact, I find the way most Afrikaners in South Africa live to be racist. They have contact with other kinds of people only when it comes time to have their clothes ironed or their soil tilled. And then they call us racist because we have chosen to live with others who want their children to learn the Afrikaans language and the long tragic history of Afrikaner humiliation and colonial resistance? They call us racist because we want to celebrate our holidays and practice our religion, and live among the elect who have chosen likewise? *Ach*, man.

With a smack of his palm against his armchair, he pleated his body back into position and gathered himself together for a long silent moment. I sipped my tea and looked at my notes. Already I had learned that peppering the Oranians with questions would not be the best way to learn about them. All I needed to do was show up, stay quiet, and record. Given enough time they would lose themselves in justifications. Once again Tom's selection of me as a reporter for this story made sense, though it had seemed cruel at the time.

A young boy in a blue T-shirt and a diaper picked his way into the room. The child had blond hair and blue eyes and porcelain skin; he would have been H. F. Verwoerd's reason for believing, I am certain, and had the prime minister lived to meet his great-great-grandson, he may have even believed in the child's twisted limbs and habit of whispering sotto voce in a language none could understand. I don't know the name of the child's exact condition, but he couldn't walk. Instead he crawled and clambered and twisted and tumbled, using furnishings and people to propel his body until he reached his destination. As he moved he whispered loudly, so we seemed to be listening to the approach of a coal-burning train. I put down my teacup. Boshoff IV must have felt my fright, but rather than saying anything about our visitor, he asked me about my experience in Orania.

I trust you've seen that we're human, not just a bunch of lunatics out here in the desert, he said.

I told him that most people had been polite and helpful. I told him about the farmer.

His face soured. I apologize for him, he said. Not everyone has an expansive idea of what we're doing here. Unfortunately there are people like that farmer everywhere, in the rest of South Africa, in the States, too. Would you say that's true? I've seen some terrible videos of the race struggle in the States. Things that made my skin burn.

I agreed with him that it was true.

A dreamy, faraway look drifted into his eyes as he began to speak again. I'm glad you told me about that farmer, he said. It reminds me that there's still a need for civic education when people move here. We must explain to people what our mission is, in the largest sense, so that they can utilize the Afrikaner siege mentality in a constructive way. Most Afrikaners, if they have any scrap of consciousness, have a siege mentality. The Afrikaner has been under siege for the entirety of his existence in this country. All he knows is struggle and fear, the fear that comes from being surrounded by your enemies on all sides. So the Afrikaners continue to cry out for liberation through self-rule, and this is not the first time. You remember the Boer War. Our past is still with us. The Afrikaner has always shared in the poverty and disenfranchisement of this country, and this is a trend that has accelerated since the beginning of democracy. I'm not talking about which group in this country has the most swimming pools and BMWs, miss. I'm talking about crucial material interests like education and language— *Carel.*

The boy was climbing on my legs. From the fireplace he had mounted a stool, crawled across the tile floor, and gripped my calf. He seized my knees, grabbed the arms of my chair, and was settling into my lap when his father pried him away. The child whimpered at the intrusion; he stared at me with baleful eyes and spoke to his father sharply, in pidgin Afrikaans. Boshoff IV cradled him in his arms and whispered in his ear until the boy was calm. Then he lifted his head but avoided my eyes. He rocked the child, and in the tautness of his mouth and the slow sightless blinking of his eyes I glimpsed that prideful restraint, which was all that was sustaining him, all that had sustained him, for more years than I dared guess. Excuse him, miss, Boshoff IV said crisply. He's just friendly. His voice broke here, and while I would have liked to have smiled and played with the child, I couldn't bear what was on his father's face. So I turned my gaze away.

While Boshoff IV rocked back and forth, singing softly, I sat back in my chair and listened. And as I closed my eyes I saw my past in front of me. I watched the images drift by in calm silence. And as I saw myself, my brother, my father, and my mother it dawned on me that I already knew what was to become of Carel Boshoff IV. He had moved to Orania because he believed it was the only place he could save his family through education, through language, through history. No matter his success, I knew Orania would disappoint him. I knew his family would disappoint him. He did not yet understand what it costs to ask such things of a home and a family and therefore I couldn't tell him of what remains after the cost has come due. I opened my eyes and looked at the child in his arms. Limbs knotted, mouth murmuring, eyes big, Carel Boshoff V stared back at me beyond his father's shoulder. I hope that he will be the one to tell his father what remains when the time comes—when he is of age, and he leaves Orania for his own survival.

WHEN I RETURNED from Orania I told Tom that it was time for me to leave South Africa.

I needed to make peace with California, I said, and not abdicate the dreams that had been built by my family members. I said that I had felt betrayed for years by the state's toxic exceptionalism and all the broken promises that came with it, but instead of fleeing, I needed to test what lay within my power to achieve there. I said that I felt calm and sure for the first time in my life.

Tom listened to all of this with his great reserves of patience. When I was finished, he responded with a grave nod. He looked as though he knew something that I didn't know, and I'm sure that he did.

But Tom was wise enough to know that the younger generation must make new mistakes in order to come to the same conclusions as their elders, and that through this constant and meaningless repetition of folly human progress will remain the greatest of our civilization's self-delusions. Besides, my departure offered him a good excuse for a party. And with the indispensable help of his wife, Gina, Tom sent me off in grand style.

He lived with his family in a tremendous ranch-style home behind an industrial cement wall and an electrified gate in one of Cape Town's best neighborhoods. Inside the wall, a ring of tall, slender cypress trees, doubtless imported, surrounded the home and grounds, so not until I had identified myself on the intercom and received clearance to drive in did I see the house, with its windows ablaze and its doorbell glowing brightly, and feel comforted by the existence of others.

I walked through the house, where every lamp was lit as if to defend the inhabitants from the thick, creeping shadows of the outdoors, and admired their handiwork. The two oak dining tables were set with antique china, cut crystal, and Moroccan tablecloths. From the kitchen, the smells of grilled tri-tip steak and carmelized onion wafted through the air. Two of Tom's sons, who had the best manners of any teenagers I have ever known, greeted guests at the door. There was hand-milled lavender soap in the guest bathroom, a fully stocked bar in the study, and a women's cabaret troupe to which Gina belonged that broke out occasionally in bawdy musical numbers. With such distractions to contend with, I suppose I should not be too hard on myself for losing track of my friend Keith. He had come in stealthily, dressed in gray pants and a voluminous caftan I had never seen before, and I introduced him to several guests before sailing away on the wave of the party. Tom wandered past me with a drink in his hand and a saxophone dangling from a strap around his neck. I asked him how he had filled a room with an executive from the new ANC-opposition Democratic Party and several former revolutionaries from the days of apartheid and kept everyone laughing. They've been in politics long enough to understand who their real enemies are, Tom said. Dinner was served, and I was still musing on that comment as Gina passed out the wedges of fruit tart and the silver pots of coffee. When I had finished eating, I excused myself for a bit of air. I found Keith in the study, crawling on Tom's Turkish rugs.

I walked up, and he began to alternately howl and whisper. At first I was confused. I had seen Keith drunk, but nothing like this. Perhaps he had mixed the wrong forms of alcohol, or perhaps he was just distraught at what was for him an occasion for emotion. Or perhaps he simply felt that he was not among his audience. I don't know. What I do know is that he began to crawl out of the study's sliding doors into the backyard and in the direction of the swimming pool. I shouted for help. With a team of three guests we got a thrashing Keith indoors and confined to a couch. He calmed down and stared up at the faces hovering over him until, with many misgivings and much discussion, they left. I noticed a few suspicious shadows still hovering in from the door. If Keith noticed he chose to ignore them. I sat on an armchair as Keith lay still on the couch. I asked him what he wanted, and he told me he wanted me to take it.

Take what? I said.

Take it all, he said with a sudden contortion that nearly sent him tumbling off the couch. You must take everything you have seen here and all that we have done. You're going to need it where you're going. Nothing will be the same.

Keith—

Don't lose it, he said with such urgency that I shrunk back in my seat. Don't let it all go like I know you want to. For now you have seen what it is to live among the strangers who have become your countrymen, now you know what they have lost in exchange for the cheap consolations they believe will save their lives or souls. And you're going to have to start all over again with nothing but what you carry out of here.

I wanted to interrupt Keith, to protest or request or at least attempt to soothe his growing sense of torment. But each time a muffled noise sounded from the depths of my armchair, he heaved a great breath and launched into his message again, more distraught than ever. At last I closed my eyes and leaned my head back. Keith's words came to me from a distance that stretched further and further away—appropriate, I knew, since in fact he was not speaking to me at all but to some version of himself who may have long since departed from us.

But I knew, too, that this outburst was Keith's parting gift for me, since he thought I would need some beautiful piece of the past to which I could cling when I returned to a home changed quickly and irrevocably and possibly not for the best. As I listened to Keith I prayed that enough would remain for both of us. I sat there until the lights in the house dimmed and I could hear, ever so faintly, the sleepy chirp of birds as they gathered outside on the lawn.

ACKNOWLEDGMENTS

THROUGHOUT THIS PROJECT I was fortunate to have not only a superb editor but an ideal reader in Scott Moyers. Scott, I can't thank you enough for the intellect, the precision, and the exuberance that you brought to this book. All authors should have such an experience.

The entire team at The Penguin Press deserves similar accolades. Top to bottom, I've received nothing but patience, professionalism, and personal attention. What a cracker!

My agents, Frank Scatoni and Greg Dinkin, have shown constant faith in me. Thank you both so much for the opportunities, the savvy, and the good cheer.

A couple of other geniuses read or listened to portions of this book at different stages and offered sage advice on what to keep and what to throw out, and I'm so glad that they did. Thank you Brandon Walston, Ellis Cose, and Max Hirsh. Also thank you to Miles Marshall Lewis for his unflagging support.

The genesis of this book is a conversation I had with the great Anthony Walton. Although what emerged is nothing like the idea he offered, he was kind enough to calm me at many moments during the process. Thank you for inspiring me not only with this book, but also with the outrageous idea that it's still possible to be a writer in these times.

In a similar vein, two professors at Harvard gave me the space and the sensibility to grow within literature: Werner Sollors and Phillip Fisher. Without their optimism and patience, I might not have found within myself the confidence to write this. And without the support and guidance I got from Sandy Close and Nell Bernstein, I might not have found within myself the possibility.

Some dear friends helped me in ways that, though not literary, were no less important: They called to check on me, they got me out of the house on occasion, and they kept me from flying off the rails. Elie Ernest, Chris West, Alicia Fenner, David Maynier, Nirmala Nataraj—you're all dazzlers, and I love you.

Many of the names in this book have been changed, but the people behind them are no less real and no less deserving of my appreciation—for all of the lessons they offered me, good and bad. As for my family, their courage continues to amaze me. My mistakes are my own, guys, but my achievements belong to you.